10/2

TO LOVE A CHILD

TO LOVE A CHILD

CHILD

NANCY REAGAN

WITH JANE WILKIE

THE BOBBS-MERRILL COMPANY, INC.
INDIANAPOLIS / NEW YORK

Library of Congress Cataloging in Publication Data

Reagan, Nancy, 1923-
To love a child.

1. Foster grandparent program. I. Wilkie, Jane.
II. Title.
HV875.R34   362.7'33   82-15277
ISBN 0-672-52711-1   AACR2

Published by The Bobbs-Merrill Co., Inc.
Indianapolis/New York
Manufactured in the United States of America

Designed by Jacques Chazaud
First Printing

This book is dedicated to the Foster Grandparents of America, who truly know how to love a child.

I would like to thank Jane Wilkie, who traveled America for me interviewing foster grandparents for possible inclusion in this book. She was of invaluable help in preparing this manuscript.

CONTENTS

CONTENTS

FOREWORD

About the Foster Grandparent Program . . .

These are people I love.

They are the elderly who have refused to knuckle under to the evening of their years. Instead, they have gotten out of their homes, out of rocking chairs—indeed, even out of their sickbeds—to minister to the ill-starred young. Age has not been a deterrent. Even Pearl Williams, who was not certain when she died in October of 1981 whether she was 111 or 112 years old, enriched the last nine years of her life as a foster grandmother.

It is my misfortune that I have not met all of the "grandparents" in this book. As First Lady I have much less freedom to travel than I did as wife of California's governor, and so, while I have known many of them, I now know the majority only through the letters that pour into my office in The White House.

The letters come from the foster grandparents themselves as well as from the 233 project directors of the FGP across the land and beyond the older borders—Puerto Rico, the Virgin Islands, Alaska, and Hawaii. They tell of the continuing successes of the old working with the young, and the stories in this book are those I've found so touching, so inspiring that they are sealed into my memory.

It was in California, when my husband was governor,

that I first learned of the Foster Grandparent Program. A doctor's daughter, I'd always been in the habit of visiting hospitals, and the day in 1967 I went to Pacific State Hospital in Pomona, I was immediately captivated by a small boy. George was an Oriental, perhaps nine years old, and the fact he was hydrocephalic didn't put a dent in his strength. He took one look at me, grabbed my hand, and didn't let go for most of that day. He tugged me up and down halls, into and out of rooms. Both the state security people and George's foster grandfather, a dear man named Roscoe, were concerned and asked if I didn't want George removed from the end of my arm. By this time George's adoring glances had endeared him to me and I said no, so he took me through the hospital and even out into the street. George cried when I left. I did, too.

I was told that day of the Foster Grandparent Program, a program that used volunteer elderly to care for mentally retarded children. I couldn't wait to tell Ronnie about it, and he agreed with me that here was a program unusual in that it was beneficial in *two* directions—the caring and the cared for.

I've worked ever since to expand the FGP. When it was picked up by ACTION, the volunteer service agency, it received increased funds and, ultimately, the children involved included the blind, the deaf, those physically handicapped, kids with language disorders and with specific learning disabilities. As it grew, it included children who have been abused or neglected, juvenile offenders, and those in need of other kinds of foster care.

The FGP is my baby, and my involvement during the past fifteen years has been like watching my child grow up. When I first learned of the FGP, there were sixty-three projects with 2,000 grandparents and 6,000 children. Now there are over 18,000 grandparents serving over 54,000 children on any given day. Perhaps because of my early interest in the program, California has been extraordinarily receptive to it; while the average project sponsor contributes 20 percent to the federal program's cost, California funds 60 percent of its FGP project. California's program has been expanded from the Pacific State Hospital to all nine state hospitals and from 150 grandparents to today's 750.

But enough of statistics—and boasting about the growth of the program. Let me tell you *why* I think it is so great.

I think it's a success because it relies in the main on the wondrous rapport between widely separated generations. There is something about the love of grandparents that transcends the parent/child relationship; it seems a fact of nature that the very young and the very old cannot resist the warmth offered each to the other. In a way, it restores the family unit that is the strength of our country. I often think how sad it is for all of us that the splintering of family has been on the increase in America. Offspring leave home after completing their education, often to marry and establish a life far from their loved ones. As a result, their children grow up without the joy of grandparents, and vice versa. In the old days, American homes automatically included grandparents, and sometimes a great-aunt or great-uncle or two. And the old folks were always there to bandage a scraped knee, inflate a balloon, lay gentle hands on the tousled heads of the children.

My own paternal grandmother, Anne, was a woman I adored. Although my parents had separated when I was born, my grandmother was not about to forfeit her only grandchild, and I was the beneficiary of her love until her death just before I was married. At the age of six I was given a set of brand-new grandparents, when my mother married a second time. Dr. Loyal Davis, the man I've always considered my own father, had parents in Galesburg, Illinois. Grandfather Davis was a railroad engineer for the Burlington line, and he built a playhouse for me in their back yard. Grandmother Davis was a splendid cook, and I loved my summer visits to their home. Both of them put up with my devotion to producing plays in that same back yard, and as I look back, I'm sure they were instrumental in producing audiences for those amateur afternoons that meant so much to me.

Foster grandparents must be in good health and at least sixty years old when they start in the program. Many have reached that point in their lives when they feel un-loved, unneeded, unwanted—all the things no one wants to feel. The children, on the other hand, need a great deal of love and attention—more than any hospital can provide. When you bring these two groups together, each gives to the other what is needed, and it is a wondrous sight to behold. The grandparents are given a whole new life, a reason for getting up in the morning, a purpose for living; and the children are the recipients of all that extra love and understanding.

Many of the highly trained professionals on staffs of FGP projects at institutions now admit that, at the start, they harbored a lot of misgivings about the "intrusion" of these people who were to come and help with the children. These old folks, said the pros, had no training in child behavior, no understanding of the vernacular of the social workers and psychologists working at the program centers. The elderly could only be interested, reasoned the professionals, because of the tax-free hourly stipend paid for their services, small as it was. Or perhaps, because low-income people were accepted as foster grandparents, they liked the idea of the daily free hot meal or the annual physical examination, also free. Whatever the lure, the old folks were certain to get in the way, to be excess baggage.

These professional doubting Thomases soon turned into believers, however. There's one story concerning a deeply disturbed boy who one day was wholly uncontrollable. His tantrum was so violent, so powerful that no one on the trained staff could think of an accepted procedure to calm him. Yet when the child's foster grandmother walked into the room where the boy was thrashing about, she simply sat there, in silence. Quite soon the tantrum was over, and those with college degrees could only shake their heads in wonder, smile, and be grateful.

While the grandparents are trained during their orientation to follow staff orders, they have been known to rise to occasional disagreement and say to the pro, "Don't you tell me what she can't do!" It is this spirit that has so often resulted in handicapped children learning to walk, talk, feed and dress themselves, and sometimes even return to normal life, a goal often deemed impossible by the professionals—a group that has learned fast about the "old folks."

A staff member involved in a Maine project says, "We don't say that every time an older person opens his or her mouth wisdom pours out. But there's a certain perspective. They look back and see things we can't see. Everything takes time. And they have been through time . . ."

What holds it all together is the love and support that comes from the feeling of family. I learned how important this is from a good friend of mine, a Jewish woman of Hungarian birth who had been incarcerated at Dachau, Belsen *and* Auschwitz. It was an unspoken horror between us; she never mentioned it, until the time of the Bay of Pigs, when she became frightened by the new threat of oppression and spilled out her story to me. The Nazis had killed her grandparents and her younger brother. The Nazis had a sound reason, she told me, for separating families within the concentration camps. They had learned that prisoners with family around them could endure suffering with much greater strength than when placed among strangers. And so they split up the family groups. Her story fortifies my belief, my faith, in the importance of the family unit.

What of the children in the program? They have been the abandoned, the forgotten, the victims of pernicious neglect. They range in age from infancy to twenty-one years. Approximately half have parents who know their whereabouts—but only half of those are visited by their mothers and fathers. I confess I cannot understand parents who do not visit their institutionalized children. Perhaps it is because parents cannot bear facing the fact their own child cannot recognize them. Perhaps it is too painful in some other way.

The foster grandparents harbor no such feelings. Their impetus for spending hours with "their" children is love, pure and simple. The fact that it is doubly beneficial is one reason the cost of the program is so worthwhile. The energy and talent of our senior citizens is a great but often untapped natural resource of our country. Not too long ago a cost/benefit study by a top management consulting firm was made of the FGP, with the conclusion that "it would be difficult to find a federal program as productive as the Foster Grandparent Program."

I have still another reason to think it a sound idea, and that is because it encourages the spirit of volunteerism. Our country has reached its heights in great part because of the willingness of Americans to contribute. I shall never fail to be amazed at the innate *goodness* of Americans. They have only to read of a tragedy, of a need, of someone crying out for help, and they immediately offer a hand.

And so I work to encourage those past sixty years of age, with low incomes and in good health, to become foster grandparents. I tell them of the small stipend the funding can afford, and I sometimes tell them of a possible fringe benefit. I tell of the time I visited a project in Phoenix and was suddenly aware of an unusual flurry. It seemed I'd arrived on a day all the grandparents were celebrating the wedding of a grandfather and a grandmother who'd met because of their participation in FGP. There have been other romances since, but these two old smoothies had *eloped*, a bit of news that made my day!

I speak to foster grandparents as often as I can, and, thank goodness, they speak to me. They tell me, "My Tommy fills my life" . . . "After my wife died I began turning into a vegetable—until this" . . . "Carmen has taught me how to have fun again. When no one is looking, I slide down the slide with her" . . . "The empty days are full again. I can't wait to come to work each morning."

One woman told me that when she awoke after open-heart surgery, the first thing she did was to question her doctor about when she could get back to her "grandchildren." The doctor had said her love for them was the reason for her recovery.

Many work with youthful offenders whose records often make the grandparents feel threatened—until they come to know and understand their charges. Many more work with severely retarded children; their faded eyes light with such love as they look at a hydrocephalic child or a child with Down's syndrome, and then turn to me and say, "I want you to meet my grandchild. Isn't she beautiful?"

At times like these I find it most difficult not to cry. I weep easily, which can be embarrassing sometimes. My husband calls it my "puddling" and teases that I cry if I have to send out the laundry—but of course I can't let a tear escape when I'm with my grandparents and the children.

So it is a luxury to come across something such as the following, and just let myself puddle in private. What provokes my weepiness is what I hear from the project directors, the sort of stories that make up the body of this book. Here, for instance, is what happened between Grandma Penrose and Bruce at the Duvall Home for Mentally Retarded Children in Glenwood, Florida. Bruce is mentally handicapped as well as blind, yet he learned from Georgia Penrose how to read Braille. She taught him many things, including the story of Hellen Keller. Then one day Bruce said he would like to dictate his thoughts, if Grandma Penrose would please write them down for him.

Here is what Bruce called *Helen Keller and I*:

> Helen Keller wrote a book called *Three Days to See*.
>
> I guess if I had my eyesight for three days I would see shadows, stores, and people. I would walk outside and look at my friends.
>
> I think I would like to play baseball. I would be the catcher and play big-league baseball.
>
> I would go to school and do puzzles.
>
> I would drive a car down the street.
>
> I am lucky, though. I can hear, and Helen Keller could not. I can read Braille like she did. I can tell who people are by their voices or their footsteps. I can dress myself and blow bubbles.
>
> Maybe God had a reason for making me this way.
>
> Bruce McDougal

I end this foreword with a prayer that God give a special blessing to all those involved in the Foster Grandparent Program.

Nancy Reagan

The White House
August, 1982

MARY

In a room at the Wassaic Developmental Center in New York's Dutchess County, Mary Wright sits at a table with a blind and mentally retarded child. On the table is a box filled with large round and tubular wooden beads, all pierced by a narrow hole. The child holds a braided string in one hand and with the other takes the wooden bead handed her by Mary and after locating the hole by touching it with her tongue, threads it onto the string. As the child succeeds with a yellow bead, Mary smiles and hands her a red one.

Mary is a large and handsome woman, her glowing skin the color of sable, her voice deep and musical. She does not look her seventy-four years; the one sign of age is the streak of white hair to the left of center at her forehead. Mary Wright is also blind. How does she know when the child has strung another bead?

"I hear it," Mary says. "I hear things now I never could hear before."

Why does the child locate the hole in the bead with her tongue?

"The tongue has the best tactile sense of any part of the body."

Mary has been blind only two years, and in that time period she has learned a quantum of things. The trauma began after she turned seventy and had retired after twenty years of working with emotionally disturbed children. The problem seemed to be her glasses; Mary just didn't see as clearly as she used to, and she went to a doctor about it. He told her she had been right. Her eyes were healthy, and all she needed was new glasses. The new ones made things just as blurry as the old pair, and Mary went back to him. He made a change in the lens prescription, but she still couldn't see clearly. He then sent her to a specialist who ruled out glaucoma. Two years went by before Mary was seen by an opthalmologist who diagnosed glaucoma.

"I'm sorry," he said. "I'll start treatment, but I'm afraid it's too late. I wish I had seen you earlier, Mary."

In the months during which her sight grew dimmer, Mary fought the increasing blindness. At first she denied it. It couldn't be, it *wouldn't* be. Next year she'd be able to drive the car again. Finally she had to accept it; she was bumping into things in the house and was unable to find things she dropped on the floor.

When she faced the reality that she was in fact going to be blind, she sank into deep depression. Neighbors noted that she was "snappish" and difficult to talk to. Actually, Mary didn't want anyone around; she wanted to be alone. Day after day she sat in the living room of her small house, refusing to see worried friends. There was no family to visit. Mary had been widowed twice, both deaths having occurred many years ago, and fate hadn't seen fit to give her children.

As the sun set each day and the house grew dark, Mary told herself that was the way it would be all the time: dark. She wouldn't be able to drive, to go anywhere, wouldn't even be able to plant a garden. She loved the outdoors and always had. As a child in South Carolina, she had hurried through her household chores to run outside and work with plants and trees. If she couldn't even go outdoors, she might as well be dead. Mary considered how to commit suicide. No jumping out of windows, she might injure someone else. She had no garage for her car, so carbon monoxide was out. She didn't know anything about guns and wouldn't have the nerve to stab herself.

She sat and rocked and thought. She was approaching the age of seventy-two and didn't have long to live anyway; she might as well use this time to plan her funeral. She asked a neighbor to drive her to the undertaker and left the house for the first time in weeks.

"Would you like to see the different caskets?" asked the unctuous funeral director.

"No, I don't want to *see*," said Mary. The very word was becoming like a knife in her heart. "I don't care what color it is."

But she picked out a casket, chose a service, paid for it all, and returned to her house, where she put on her robe and sat by the window and waited to die.

Looking back on that period in her life Mary says now, "Nothing happened, of course. I didn't even get a headache." She smiles slightly at the memory. "When I realized I couldn't just sit there, perfectly healthy except for my eyes—and that I didn't have the courage to kill myself—I phoned my doctor and asked him to put me in touch with someone who could help me. He gave me the number of an agency in White Plains and told me he would send them my records. First they sent a social worker, and then two counselors came to work with me. They were wonderful. When I kept saying I couldn't do this or that they'd say 'Yes you can. We're right here. We won't let you hurt yourself.' They came to my house once a week, and they really pulled me out of it."

One of the men, the mobility guide, made Mary put on

a blindfold and go outdoors in utter darkness. The other helped her with guidance on methods of cooking and cleaning and everyday living in general.

"But I can't stay indoors in nice weather," she said. "How can I plant flowers when I can't see?"

"If you learn Braille you'll be able to do everything you've ever done, except drive a car," said the counselor. "You want to plant a garden? Here, I'll show you how."

He told her to get on her knees in the soil and tie a string on a stake in the center of the spot where she wanted her flowers. Then holding the end of the string, she made a circle in the soil with a finger and planted the seeds. She made two flower beds and then a vegetable garden. She grew broccoli, tomatoes, green peppers all that summer and put some in a freezer. Doing things she'd been accustomed to doing improved her attitude. Maybe she really could still enjoy life.

The counselors helped enormously but Mary's own background, as well as her intelligence, were greatly responsible for her emotional recovery. With her second husband she had been given a foster child she loved dearly. But with her husband's death in 1954, Mary had to surrender the child; the law stated that foster children could not be given to people living alone. But the same agency then asked Mary to work for them in child care, and she began her vocation of working with emotionally disturbed children. With twenty years of experience, she was aware of things like mental depression and familiar with the work of psychiatrists. "It didn't take me too long to pull out of it," she says, "because I sort of knew what to do after I recognized the fact I was in a depression. I worked at it, made myself do things."

By the time the counselors had finished with her, Mary was ready to get out and live again. And when they learned of her experience in working with children, they recommended the Foster Grandparent Program. Mary joined in the autumn of 1981, at which time her sight was completely gone in the left eye and only occasional shadows could be seen with the right.

But she had been given time to prepare for blindness and to work toward life without sight and had learned so many things. Making up for loss of sight, other senses were sharpened. In cooking, for example, hearing became a marvel. Mary had thought she knew all there was to know about cooking. After all, when she was growing up in the South, the eldest of seven children, she had begun cooking when she was so little she had to stand on a stool to see what was on top of the stove. But now that she could no longer see, she learned she could *hear* food cooking. "Raw, half cooked, or done, it sounds different," she says. "You have to listen, and you'll know when things are done."

When her flowers began to bloom, she discovered for the first time that each kind of flower has a different feel. She can differentiate among them by touching a petal or a leaf.

"When I had my sight I never noticed so many things," she says. "Someone asked me yesterday how I get dressed, how I know what colors to put on, and I told her there is a difference in the way every piece of clothing feels."

To the blind children at the Wassaic Center, Mary Wright is a jewel. She passes on to them her own sensations, knowledge, experiences. "It's mostly talking to them. I let them know they are not alone, that another blind person has made it and that they can, too. They try walking across a room and put their hands to their faces to protect them. They have to learn. We have kids here who are not only blind, but they can't hear or speak either. And these youngsters experience by picking up vibrations. They don't want to sink into darkness alone, they want someone there with them, and if grandma can just sit there and hold their hand, it's often enough. I had one little boy—I put some lotion on his hands and massaged them, and when I took my hand away, he would reach out and grab it. They just need to know someone is there, and touch is so important.

"This program has been a lifesaver for me. I'm so glad to be able to work with the blind and help them through a difficult time. I understand. I've been there."

She has the savvy for the work as well as the patience. Mary knows enough, for instance, to stand to the side of the blind children, not in front of them, because in their frustration they often strike out suddenly. She encourages the blind who are afraid to move to get up and walk. She influences those who don't like to use their hands to play drums, anything to make them use their hands. This will be particularly important when they begin learning Braille, and it is Mary who teaches them. She enrolled in a correspondence course after joining the Foster Grandparent Program, and when her grades were sent, she was ecstatic to learn she'd been given an A plus.

"To be able to read again is like being reborn. I've always loved to read. It has been my hobby, and I've had to give up so many books I loved and was planning to read in the future. Learning Braille—just being blind—is like going back to school, because I'm learning so many new things. Braille takes sighted people about a year to learn, or so they tell me. I think I'm going to read it quite easily in less than a year, not because I'm smarter, but because I *have* to learn it and sighted people don't."

Teaching Braille to the kids is her joy. It depends, of course, on a child's intelligence, but Mary insists that if a youngster can learn the English alphabet, he can learn Braille. It takes longer, but then everything with the disturbed and the retarded takes longer, and Mary has the time.

Not long ago a friend, concerned over Mary's advanced age, combined with her living alone and having no family, asked Mary how she viewed the future. Had she thought about what she might do as the years roll onward? Mary Wright didn't waste a second in answering—nor did she correctly interpret her friend's question.

She said, "Oh, the future will be fine. Because if anything happens to the Foster Grandparent Program, God forbid, I'll do some other kind of volunteer work. You know, be with people, help people."

ROBERT

On January 13, 1979, in Montgomery City, Missouri, farmer Robert Powell was eating his dinner. In his sixty years he had never married, and so he was alone. The newspaper was propped on the table, and while reading it he reached for his knife to cut another piece of pork chop. His hand, the right hand, refused to come up from his lap to the table. Puzzled, Robert looked at his right arm and said, "Come on, what's the matter with you?"

The matter was that he had just suffered a stroke, the first of two. The second, which took place the following day in a hospital, was a major seizure. With that one, Robert's entire right side was paralyzed, and his speech was badly impaired. After a battery of tests he was told he had a brain tumor that must be removed immediately.

By that time Robert had regained his speech—an early sign of the valor and determination of the man—and so when they told him after the surgery that he would never walk again or use his right hand again, he looked at them without a hint of a smile. "Never tell me never. Never is a long time." He looked at the outline of his right leg beneath the sheet. "I'm gonna use that leg if I have to drag it behind me."

That was his idea and his goal, but such things are easier said than done. It was May of that year before Robert was moved to a nursing home in Columbia, Missouri. When he was allowed out of bed, he was put into a wheelchair, and he learned to propel himself with the strength of only his left arm. There were many in the nursing home worse off than he, so he counted his blessings and looked to the future.

A month or so later, the activity director of the nursing home described the Foster Grandparent Program and asked Robert if he would like to become a foster grandparent.

"How could I? I never had any kids of my own. I don't know anything about kids. Besides, I'm stuck in this danged wheelchair."

"We're thinking of bringing kids here from the day-care center down the street," he was told. "A lot of them from broken homes. You don't need to know anything about kids. We thought that bringing them to the nursing home would make things brighter for any of you who want to be a grandparent."

The FGP director in Columbia, meanwhile, had a better idea. Why not bring the grandparents from the nursing home to the day-care center?

The first day Robert was wheeled into the center he discovered a room where a small table was furnished with a saw, hammer, sandpaper, blocks, and pieces of wood. A six-year-old was attempting to use a vise and doing it all wrong.

"Here," said Robert, wheeling himself to the bench. "Let me show you how to do that."

With his background of army service in Italy and Africa during World War II, his experience in the CCC, and his lifetime of repairing all the things that break down on a farm, Robert was an old hand with all kinds of tools. And so in July of 1979 he became a full-fledged foster grandparent, teaching children about woodworking.

He discovered that kids weren't such mysterious beings after all. They were fascinated by his wheelchair, asking to push it, wanting to hitch a ride on it. The little ones, many as young as two years, milled around the chair, wanting a pat on the head from grandpa, and some of them got in the way. By this time Robert drove his wheelchair with considerable skill. "Toot, toot, you kids!" he called out. "I don't want any of you to be the first in history to be run over by a wheelchair."

"Why don't you throw that thing away?" demanded five-year-old Mike.

It was a suggestion that followed questions from a score of kids, all amounting to the same thing: "Grandpa, why can't you walk?"

A good question, thought Robert Powell. He couldn't explain "why" to the children; it is virtually impossible to describe to a child how a stroke affects the body.

By the time twenty young faces had looked up into his and asked, "Why don't you walk, grandpa?" Robert tried something new at the nursing home. Along the hall was a rail for those needing support while walking. When he thought no one was looking, Robert wheeled his chair to the end of the hall, pulled himself up and stood. Not for long; his good left leg, weakened from disuse, was not strong enough to bear his weight. But that day Robert Powell put some of his weight on his right leg. He repeated the exercise every afternoon and within weeks began standing up every couple of hours at the day-care center as well as the nursing home.

The children watched, wide-eyed. "What are you *doing?*" they wanted to know.

Nine-year-old Rick said, "Grandpa, when they operated on you, did they throw away your brain?" Robert chuckled at that; he never did know if Rick asked the question in innocence or if the boy thought Robert was crazy for getting out of his wheelchair when there weren't any grownups around to help him.

The day came when Robert could not only stand but could take a step or two. Then three. At the VA hospital, where his surgery had taken place, he hadn't been able to stand up even with support. Now he was beginning to walk. Now he was winning. The kids cheered. They grabbed his hand—the left one—to help.

A therapist saw Robert practicing in the hall of the nursing home and told him not to exert himself, because he would never walk again. "Tell you what," said Robert, "who's going to hit the door first, you or me? If you don't think I'm going to walk again, you might as well leave this place right now."

Quite naturally, the administration of the home worried that Robert would fall, perhaps break a hip. He gave them the same sort of response he had given to the therapist. "Tell you what. I'll ask the doctor, and if he doesn't say okay, then I'll just go to some other home."

He wished they could realize how much better he had felt since he had begun practicing to walk. Not only that, he was sleeping better. Before starting to work in the hall, he had wakened every hour during the night. He figured that the staff just didn't understand or that perhaps they were getting upset because Robert was encouraging all those at the home who couldn't walk to give it a try. If he could do it, he reasoned, so could they.

Within a year he was so adept that he could play games with the children. When one of the younger ones took off with his cane, Robert would groan and pretend he was going to fall, and within seconds the cane was back at his hand, three or four children having competed in the rescue.

Eighteen months following the brain surgery, Robert walked into the office of his surgeon. *Walked* in. The doctor looked up from his desk, and his mouth fell open.

Robert grinned at him. "How'm I doin'?"

The astonished doctor tested his leg, tapping for nerve reaction. There was none at the knee, thigh, calf, or ankle. "Walk back and forth for me," he said.

Robert obliged, as jauntily as possible, and the doctor scratched his head. "I don't know how you're doing it, Powell, but, however, keep on doing it."

That is more or less what all the physicians say. They can't understand how he is managing to walk.

Robert thinks it's the kids. The kids and his own determination, which is of gargantuan proportions. He has taught himself to write with his left hand and continues to work with his right arm, which has been slower to cooperate than the leg. He wears the arm in a supportive sling, and when an unthinking person reaches to shake Robert's right hand, he struggles to make it respond.

The children say that it will some day. They have seen Robert attempting to clap his hands together. He got the idea as he watched the children applauding one day and thought to himself, I can do that too. He brought his good left hand up from underneath to meet the other one and continued to smack his limp right hand.

A nearby foster grandparent said, "Have you gone crazy?"

Robert smiled. "I've got me a way to make this thing work."

He was so excited about the idea that he applied for the newly available job of assistant coordinator at the local Foster Grandparent Program. It would be working for the same director who had first thought of taking the grandparents to the day-care center, and Robert was sure he could handle it.

The director's voice was gentle. "I'm sure you could too. Except, Robert, the job requires typing ability."

"Well, I could learn. I'd learn slow, but I'd learn."

He wasn't well enough to fill the job, but he was recovering so well that he took a week's vacation back at his bachelor digs in Montgomery City to see if he could make it on his own. It didn't last a week because he couldn't clean the place properly, and there was no one to do his laundry, so he went back to Columbia and the nursing home.

"But the main reason was that I missed the kids," he says. "I couldn't stand it without them."

He was anxious to get back to his FGP job, and the first morning after his return, people in the neighborhood saw a familiar sight—Robert Powell rolling downhill in his wheelchair the distance of the block between the nursing home and the day-care center. The children's faces lit up. "Hi, grandpa!" and Robert brushed away a few tears.

In his three years with the program, as many as fifty children have experienced Robert's woodworking class. There is a considerable turnover in youngsters because of changing conditions in their homes or, in some cases, newly arrived immigrants. One little girl from Vietnam was so frightened that she cried most of the first morning at the center. Then Robert, the bachelor who thought he knew nothing about children, offered a suggestion.

"I told them I didn't think they should hold her in their arms. I said to get her a chair and sit her by the kitchen door where she can watch her mom on one side and on the other watch the kids playing. Sure enough, that settled her down. Now, you understand, this little girl couldn't speak English or understand it. But she used to come and watch other kids working in the shop, and I swear it wasn't more than a week later when she came to me and said, plain as day, 'Grandpa, I want to make an airplane.' I almost fell over; her English was that good. I showed her on a square how to make the board, and she understood right away. When she finished her little plane, she was tickled to death, and when she left three months later, she was speaking English just as good as the other kids."

Robert remembers wonderful small moments as personal victories, such as the day he visited another school and noticed a little boy who sat down and tore off his shoe and sock. When the teacher told him to put them back on, Robert said, "Wait a minute. He has a sore foot there." Sure enough, it was a blood blister, and Robert found a rough place on the inside of the shoe. They said it would take a long time to get the shoe fixed, and Robert said he'd buy a pair of shoes for the boy before all that. "Anyway," he remembers, "the boy went to the doctor and came back with a pair of sneakers on. I've always been thankful I went out there that day."

Robert was to know more illness. At the nursing home late in 1981 he felt suddenly dizzy and weak, and the upshot was a second brain operation. The evening before the operation his surgeon said to him, "You just hang in there, Mr. Powell."

"I've got to," Robert replied. "You see, I've got to get back to my grandkids."

He came out of the recovery room "a little confused," but nothing stops him for long. The next morning he asked for breakfast, and the nurses told him he wasn't well enough to eat.

"You bring my breakfast, and we'll see if I can't eat."

He cleaned the plates, of course. He was feeling so fine they sent him back to the ward. "The nurses there thought they'd decided not to operate on account of I was back so soon."

He was inundated by a flood of get-well cards and even letters from the "grandkids," and a huge poster signed by them all was tacked on the wall behind his bed.

In three weeks he was back again at the day-care center with his beloved children—and back again at the nursing home, prodding other patients there to try to walk. The result is that the nurses are occasionally finding patients at the end of the hall, out of their wheelchairs, and holding onto the railing. One is eighty-seven years old and insisting he's going to learn "the way Powell did."

In the meantime, Robert rolls down the hill every morning and thinks about the day he'll be able to walk down and maybe even walk back up.

"You know," he says, "I'm almost grateful I had that stroke. It's as though I had it just so I could take care of my kids."

MABEL

Not long after the end of the First World War, a man appeared at the door of an orphanage in southern Michigan, with a blue-eyed baby girl in his arms.

"We don't want her," he told authorities at the home. "She's feebleminded, and we can't take care of her."

In those days, the orphanage was referred to as the lunatic asylum inasmuch as the inmates were a mixture of the unwanted and the mentally deficient, some of them there simply on the word of a relative or family friend who had only to say, "Take this child."

Almost half a century later Mabel Lewis was released from that home into the outside world, on her own for the first time in her life. Twice during that time she had been moved, once for a period of five years to another institution where, as a teenager, she was sterilized; and earlier, to a foster home, which would remain a dim memory of a kindly woman who soon died of cancer, and small Mabel was shipped back to the mental home.

There, she slept in a room lined with a score of beds occupied by girls and women who could not, or would not, talk to her. There was no one to come and visit her, and she had no friends. Although there were about 200 residents in the home, no one *could* be a friend; many were blind or deaf, and few had Mabel's higher mentality.

She abided by the rules: Do not talk about what you see. If one woman mistreats another, forget it. If you squeal you will be locked up in the punishment building. If a girl appears to be pregnant, do not report it. Above all, keep quiet.

When she became an adult it was decided to allow Mabel to go "out" during weekdays and earn money for herself by doing house and yard work. She worked six days a week scrubbing in beauty shops and homes in the town of Coldwater and saved her earnings.

With some of the money she bought a radio; it had been her dream to have a small radio she could listen to on Sundays when she wasn't working. The next day, when she returned from work, she turned it on and found it wouldn't work. When it was learned another inmate had purposely damaged the radio that inmate was punished—but so was Mabel. She'd become so angry that she was sent to the punishment building overnight.

The doors were locked there, as they were through much of the institution, and Mabel chafed against this because of the contrast of her freedom during the days when she was working in the town and could walk on grass and look up at the sky. But she always came back to her bed at night. Where else was there to go? She had never known a home or a bed of her own.

Mabel had tasted freedom, and she loved it. The negative aspect was that it made her more aware of the fact she had been a prisoner all her life, and she strengthened her resolve to one day live her own life.

A step forward took place with the increase of deinstitutionalizing. Because of Mabel's record of good orientation, she was given a trial run at being on her own.

17

This time she would work as before in the town, but she would be allowed to sleep at the home of an aide who worked at the institution.

And then came the big day in 1969. She was forty-nine years old when the social worker called her in for a talk.

"You've done well, Mabel," the woman said. "You've joined a church, and you've worked hard, and we feel it's time to release you."

Despite years of dreaming about freedom, a sting of fear shot through her that day. Would she be able to make it on her own? Would people point at her and talk behind her back because she had been a mental patient?

By that time there had been two people in her life who influenced the thoughts she had that day. One was a woman who claimed a relationship and through the years had told Mabel, "You're nobody, and you'll never be anybody. You're no good." The continued putdown had depressed her deeply; it was the one thing that had discouraged her in her valiant struggle toward freedom. But there was a plus factor too. The director of the local Foster Grandparent Program whom Mabel had met at church. She often saw the woman on the grounds of the mental home, usually in the kitchen where Mabel worked, and when they stopped to talk, the woman would give her a hug. No one had ever hugged Mabel, and the warmth of human touch brought tears to her eyes. "Believe you me," she told the director, "when I get out of here and get to be sixty, I'm going to be a foster grandmother."

Much time had to pass before that birthday, and Mabel filled the years with accomplishment. With the money she had saved, she bought a three-wheeled bicycle that she still rides around town, an American flag fluttering from the handlebars and above the front wheel, a sign that reads, I LOVE GOD. She bought a trailer home, "Now mine all mine, all paid for—including insurance."

In the time required for that particular victory, Mabel achieved another. It began the day she went to clean a house for a woman she assumed was a stranger, but Mrs. Waldron looked at her so long and hard that Mabel felt uncomfortable.

"Is something the matter?"

"Don't I know you?"

"No, you don't," said Mabel.

"Oh, but I do. Didn't you live years ago up in the country in a foster-care home?"

Mabel nodded, mystified.

"And didn't you go to the one-room country school?"

"Well . . . yes."

"I was your teacher," said Margery Waldron.

She was the second friend of Mabel's life and pleaded with her to return to school and finish her education. "You can do it, Mabel, I know you can. I know all about you, that you're free now, and you can start where you left off and get your high-school diploma. I want to help."

Mrs. Waldron accompanied Mabel to buy the necessary books, and Mabel knuckled down to study in the hours she was off from work. "It was hard, mighty hard, at my age," she says. "But I did it. I got my high-school graduation papers in 1976. And then I did something else. I wanted to put a bit of spark in my life, so I went to Bible college by mail, and I did that for four years and graduated with honors."

None of it was easy, not even the simple fact of being free. As she had thought they might, people pointed her out and talked behind her back. On the day her phone was installed—a luxury for which she had saved many months—her first call was from a local woman. The voice was even: "Mabel Lewis, you get out of our church. Your presence there is giving the church a black name."

The blood seemed to rush downward into Mabel's legs. "What do you mean, a black name?"

"I'm not going to tell you what I mean, but you better leave," said this sorry example of Christianity.

Mabel tried to ignore the call. She was happy in her

church, she sang in the choir, she studied her Bible every day. And then a man's voice attacked her by phone, and it was a nasty voice: "You get out of our church, I'm warning you. If you don't get out right away you're going to be mighty sorry."

Mabel decided that the threats could not be ignored, and so she joined another church, "a sweet, dear little church," where she plays the tambourine in the band.

Yet another achievement was Mabel's final triumph over the circumstances—very possibly the mistake—that had kept her in a mental institution most of her life. Saying nothing to anyone, she approached a lawyer who agreed to take her case to probate court where she ultimately won a judgment that she was legally free and "restored to sound mind."

By this time she was accustomed to the thrill of riding her three-wheeled bike, its big basket loaded with groceries she had bought to cook for herself on her own stove, in *her* kitchen, in *her* home. But now, legally free and pronounced wholly sane, there was a new dimension. As she pedaled through the town, she held her head high. "I am a real person at last," she told herself.

On the day she turned sixty, she phoned her friend the FGP director. "Okay, here I am, old enough. I want to keep my word to you, and if you'll let me be a foster grandmother, I will do my level best to follow all instructions."

Working as a foster grandparent has not required special effort from Mabel. The fact is that she understands the mentally retarded only too well and therefore is precisely where she is needed most when she works every evening with Larry, who is retarded.

But the day she was assigned to him was one filled with terror because in order to work with the boy, she learned she would have to do her four-hour stint in the very same room where she had grown up and spent most of her life.

"I can't go in there," she said.

Memories washed over her, the years spent in the company of women who rocked endlessly in chairs or on the floor. The ones with vacant stares, the silent ones, and those who screamed and tore at their hair. A shudder ran down Mabel's spine as the thought occurred to her that if she went into that room maybe they would put her back as a patient.

"I can't do it," she said again.

"But the whole building has been renovated," said the supervisor. "Mabel, please try. That is where you are needed."

She was sweating with fear as she pushed open a door that had led to the old sleeping quarters—and discovered a totally new atmosphere. Walls had been torn down, and those still standing had been covered with fresh paint. Doors had been changed. Mabel couldn't locate where the long line of clothes lockers had been. She couldn't even pinpoint the area where the rows of beds had been. She turned and went outside into the sunshine, free of the festering bitterness and certain now there were no longer any chains to bind her.

The next day she went to work with Larry. He was twenty-one years old, his sight and hearing were impaired, and his frustration was so deep that he bit his own arms and flailed about trying to injure himself.

Mabel held his arms, calmed him, kissed him. She invented games to take his mind from himself, for it was only then that Larry ceased his attempts at self-injury. She found that when she read to him he would put his head down on a table and go to sleep at the sound of her voice. She guided his hand over a multitude of wooden pegs and a board filled with holes—and made out a daily report of the number of pegs Larry had succeeded in placing into the holes. The count is now up to 900 a day. He seems reassured by holding Mabel's hand. Before she entered his life he had never been known to smile or laugh. He does both now. It had been said that no one could work with Larry, that it would be impossible. Mabel, who ought to know, said, "Nothing is impossible!"

She works with Larry in the evenings because much of the daytime is taken up with helping a neighbor who has been ill. This adds up to caring for two adults, and Mabel often wishes there were little children in her life. There is no way she could now become a mother, even if she were not beyond child-bearing years; there is the fact of her having been sterilized.

Her maternal instinct, still strong, is bestowed on her cat, the first pet Mabel has ever been able to own. Not surprisingly, she has named it "Baby."

AUDREY

Audrey Bessa wasn't at all sure about it. She'd had four of her own, and they'd all been born perfect, as had her seven grandchildren. But she had to face the truth that after ten years as a widow there wasn't anything to do any more. In particular, there were no more babies to take care of, and Audrey adored babies. She'd even planned having her own brood spaced widely apart so that she could give all her attention to one child at a time. Now even the grandchildren were growing up—the youngest was already three years old.

The idea of becoming a foster grandparent had been swimming about in her head for a year. She'd been fifty-nine when she first learned of the FGP at a booth at the Orange County Fair, so there were many months to make her decision. The drawback was simply that she didn't know if she could take the tragedy of these children with twisted minds and bodies. Audrey had never known a mentally retarded or physically handicapped child, and she was sure that just at the sight of them she would collapse in tears. That would be terrible, of course, because the children wouldn't understand why she was crying—or worse *would*, and that would be so rude.

She knew she had the physical stamina, but it was the problem of having too much sympathy—so much that she'd have to rush to the nearest restroom to cry her eyes out. If she fell apart in front of the teachers, or whatever the staff was called at the Fairview State Hospital, then maybe she'd be fired as a foster grandmother.

The hospital was a half hour away by bus from where Audrey lived in Santa Ana, California, and one day in 1974, having turned sixty and therefore eligible, she made herself travel to Costa Mesa. No one stopped her at the hospital entrance, and she found herself free to roam the grounds. She saw children propelling themselves in wheelchairs or being pushed by other children. Almost all had the look of retardation. As she approached a group of buildings, a girl of perhaps ten approached, dragging one leg encased in a brace, and threw her arms around Audrey.

"Grandma!" she said.

Audrey looked into the child's face, beaming with delight, and wondered what she should do.

"I'm not your grandmother, dear," she said.

"Oh, yes!" said the girl, and ran a hand over Audrey's white hair.

Audrey went home on the first bus to come along and cried. She couldn't do it, couldn't take the sadness of it all. If she was going to be so filled with pity, how could she possibly be of any help? But she couldn't rid her mind of the persistent awareness that these were children who needed attention, who were starving for affection. She returned twice more to the hospital, wandering the grounds and talking to the children, before she realized that when she paid them attention they were no longer sad but actually happy.

Audrey was accepted into the program, and the first two weeks she had nightmares. There was so much to do, so many places where she could help, but she was only one person. There were children all over the place at the hospital, and every one of them without a foster grandparent wanted Audrey to be theirs. Their need for love was so great. How could she spread herself that thin? It was a full month before she learned from the staff that she was going through a typical syndrome and would soon settle into a comfortable pattern.

She told the staff she'd prefer working with physically active children. "I like kids with a bit of spunk," she said. "I want to work with some that are mobile, a little bit naughtier, harder to handle. You know, kids who maybe aren't as much wanted as the others."

The staff asked if she'd be content to work only with boys, and Audrey, whose offspring are short on males (one of her four children and only one of her seven grandchildren), said that was fine with her. They took her to a room filled with boys ranging in age from eight to eighteen and suggested that she choose a grandson. They did not tell her that three other foster grandmothers had already tried working in that ward and had failed with the boys, some of whom were quite tall and strong. Audrey felt no fear as they crowded around her, every one who could talk clamoring for Audrey to choose him.

She chose the one who could not talk. Michael was sixteen and sitting in a chair at the back of the room, rocking. Rocking was all he could do. Although sighted, he was totally frustrated, unable to utter a sound.

Audrey worked with Michael for four years, finding him a boy of placid disposition who had been at Fairview since the age of four when his mother died. His father visited him regularly until he, too, died, when Michael was eight. The boy had never made a sound, and no one could recall seeing him smile. Many weeks after she had taken him for a walk every morning, he smiled at Audrey. Then when she took him to the hospital's "toy library" she was surprised by his ability to work puzzles and reported this to the staff. He strung beads without effort, he identified colors by sorting them into piles. Audrey learned that Michael's greatest joy was playing with a straw, and so she brought him a new straw every day. He began making small sounds and even hummed a little. When she took him to the fair and he saw dozens of people sipping through straws, he was in straw heaven. He picked up every one he could find on the ground, and it was all Audrey could do to prevent him from jamming the whole bunch into the soda she bought him.

"It may not seem much," Audrey says of that period, "but it was better than the terrible waste of sitting in a chair and rocking back and forth. This is the most anyone can do, find a way to give them moments of happiness, to somehow make their lives fuller."

Ultimately, Michael learned to dress and undress himself, make his bed, bathe, and eat neatly. He was put to work in the "sheltered workshop" at the hospital, a place where the handicapped are paid for piece work contracted for by firms. The work is most often simple assembly, and Michael began earning his own money, which was deposited for him into a newly opened bank account.

Michael's story is one of the successes that make me so happy when I learn of the outcome. Most particularly when I can see the surroundings in my mind's eye. Fairview was one of the hospitals I visited many times when my husband was governor of California, and I remember that while I was there a couple did the polka for me. It was the first time I was ever danced *to*.

When Michael turned twenty-one he was so able to care for himself that he was placed in a foster home. The social worker who took him there reported that the woman living in the home had placed a doughnut and a cup of cocoa on the kitchen table the morning of his arrival. When Michael walked in and was asked if he'd like the doughnut and cocoa, he pulled up a chair by himself, sat down to eat, and when he finished, picked up his dishes and put them in the sink.

"He's going to be just fine," the woman told the social worker. "It's as if he's come home."

That was almost five years ago, and Audrey Bessa hasn't seen him since. She has permission to visit him, but in her wisdom knows it is better if she does not. "For his sake, it's best," she says.

Audrey thinks one of the good things about being a foster grandmother is that she's never out of work. When Michael left, she was assigned to Bobby. Or rather *asked* for Bobby. Another boy who could not make sounds, he had been bullied by the others, and the first time Audrey saw him he was bruised and bloodied because he hadn't been able to cry out for help when another boy struck him. Bobby was stubborn, which suited Audrey just fine; under Audrey's care he rediscovered his voice and learned to speak a few words—and was no longer bullied by the other boys.

When he turned twenty-one he was transferred to another residence at the hospital, and now, four years later, when he sees Audrey on the grounds, he comes to her and puts his hand in hers. Once in a while a staff member will scold Bobby for this, until Audrey explains that she had been his foster grandmother. She feels good about Bobby, knowing he can now take care of himself and that the staff is kind to him.

Of all her boys, Audrey is proudest of Mark, a freckle-faced nineteen-year-old with red hair. When she took him on, Mark was seventeen and adrift because his foster grandmother had recently had a stroke and died. At the time, Audrey had completed a course in mental retardation and wanted a boy with a specific problem. The staff suggested Mark who, because of his love for animals, repeatedly ran away from classes to the farm on the hospital grounds. Audrey solved that by simply taking him to the farm to feed the animals before classes began.

Because Mark hasn't the ability to learn to read, Audrey is teaching him the meaning of signs, the kind of signs he'll need to understand if he goes out into the world: "Stop," "One Way," "Walk," etc. His vocabulary is limited, and he says only enough to make himself understood. Audrey goes to his classes with him now and is helping to structure his language so that he can speak in complete sentences.

"Mark is a hero to the little kids because he can tie their shoelaces," she says. "When school isn't in session, the little ones come to him from all over the grounds and hold out a foot. That's wonderful for him—he understands he can do something that they can't."

Interestingly, Mark seems to have innate good manners; if he sees a woman standing, he brings a chair to her. He shows his affection for all the foster grandparents in his own way. Whenever he sees another boy misbehaving toward a foster grandmother, Mark grabs the offender's shirt collar at the nape of the neck and his trousers at the belt and holds him until a hospital aide can take over.

Audrey's relationship with Mark is close; when the boy's parents lived for two years in another city because of the father's work, they told Audrey they had faith that she would watch over Mark while they were gone. During that period Audrey joined the Senior Volunteer Program specifically so that she would be allowed to take Mark to her own home on weekends. He so enjoyed these visits that when Audrey was ill and absent from the hospital for a few days, he started out to walk to her home. He knew the way because he had walked the route with Audrey after she moved to Costa Mesa. But he knew nothing about traffic. It was a frightening lesson, and Audrey has ceased taking him to her home until he learns and understands all the traffic signs and signals.

During the eight years Audrey has been in the program, she has noticed a touch of jealousy in the eyes of her own grandchildren when she has spoken of the youngsters at the hospital. It was aggravated when she was asked to babysit for them and had to refuse because of previous commitments to the foster grandchildren. She handled this jealousy well enough, telling them she has "hands that are empty and a heart too full," so that they understood. One of her granddaughters, now sixteen, is learning sign language and when she babysits for infants teaches them the signs for milk, bottle, etc., even before they have learned to talk. Audrey figures this teenager will become a foster grandmother in another forty-four years.

Educating her own brood has been a slow process. Until they reached their teens it was difficult for them to understand what their grandmother meant when she talked of retarded children. Last year, Audrey cleaned the slate when she took her youngest granddaughter, just turned twelve, to an ice cream parlor in the company of Patrick. Patrick was Audrey's newest foster grandchild, and to celebrate his tenth birthday, she obtained permission to take him off the hospital grounds. Although a victim of Down's syndrome, he has a happy nature and was delighted with the little girl, thinking she was also from the hospital. She in turn held his hand and gave him a little gift to open when they reached the ice cream parlor. "I think she understands now," says Audrey.

So far, Audrey Bessa has been instrumental in the dramatic improvement of six low-functioning children, to the point they have been transferred from total care at Fairview Hospital to community group homes. This effects a saving to taxpayers far and above the cost of her two-dollar hourly stipend.

Audrey plans going on "forever" as a foster grandmother. "We have one grandmother who's eighty-five years old, and I'm going to do it until at least that age. Maybe by then I might be content to take kids who are confined to wheelchairs. I'm saving those milder ones for my old age."

In the meantime she counsels foster grandparents new to the program. "Please keep coming for two more weeks," she tells them. "I know you're having nightmares right now. That's because you're allowing your pity to take over. But if you keep coming, the nightmares will stop. With pity out of the way, you see, you'll be able to do marvelous things. So please stick with it. You'll fill your life if you do."

JOHN

John Bluesalt is his complete name, and he is a medicine man of the Navajo nation in northeast Arizona. He is seventy-five years old and for the past ten years has been a foster grandfather at the Shonto Boarding School, an educational facility of the Bureau of Indian Affairs. There he teaches Indian children the culture of their tribe.

John Bluesalt is a traditional Navajo in that his education has been transmitted verbally; he does not read or write. Indians do not read their lore or knowledge; they still tell it to each other, down through the ages. John Bluesalt's education is considerable, as is that of all medicine men. He has studied for many years to learn the complex culture of his tribe, all its history and the sacred knowledge of its ceremonial rites. The erudition of the red man's medicine man is much like that of the white man's Jesuit or rabbi; it requires persons of high intelligence.

Because John Bluesalt does not speak English, it has been necessary to interview him through a translator. I think his answers to four questions are well worth a chapter in this book. Here they are:

What is important for an Indian child to learn?

To be in balance with nature. To understand, appreciate, and be proud of his identity. To know well his clanship, language, and history.

How do you contribute as a foster grandparent?

I teach the grandchildren awareness and confidence in themselves. I teach them to value education. I teach them our history and legends so they will never let our culture and traditions die. I teach them to protect our mother earth and all of nature. I teach them to respect and to love their relatives and their elders.

What do you like best about the Foster Grandparent Program?

I like the foster grandchildren and the other foster grandparents. I like to see all people my age involved. I like to be informed on issues, and I like the chance to contribute my knowledge to the young ones.

What would you like to see happen in the future?

I would like to see our children build a better society with the knowledge we pass on. I would like to see all children with special needs have a foster grandparent. I would like to have Mrs. Reagan visit our program here in Navajo Nation. A visit would encourage us and mean so much to all our foster grandparents.

I accept John Bluesalt's invitation with gratitude and humility and hereby promise him I shall make every attempt to visit the Navajo Nation in Arizona. I hope I can fulfill the promise; as First Lady I travel many places but cannot always choose my destination.

I've been enchanted by John Bluesalt's quotes and would very much like to visit him because of his enthusiasm about the Foster Grandparent Program.

Through his statements—and with a little help from his translator—I've learned something else I didn't know before. American Indians consider the FGP singularly valuable because it dovetails with so many tribal beliefs; they are surprised and pleased that an alien society has brought them an activity that relates so well to Indian culture. High among these welcome principles is the spirit of volunteerism. Long before the colonists built this country by helping one another, the Indians believed in the nobility of helping all people with hands and heart and mind. And if any have had priority, it has been the elderly and the young.

JENNIE

At Jackson Memorial Hospital in Miami they give foster grandparent Jennie Forbes the children who are dying. Jennie wants it that way.

"Somebody's got to do it," she says. "So if you know you do it the best, you'd better get to work with your giving, because then you'll know the job's well done."

Jennie has no need to apologize for the faith she professes in herself; she is convinced her ability to deal with children who are terminally ill is a gift from God. "I know he keeps me here to do this work. In the morning—if he's waked me up and let me have my good mind—I tell him I'll do what he wants. Just show me and I'll do. When I get through talkin' to him, honey, I'm on the ball!"

A buxom black woman of sixty-three, Jennie has been a foster grandmother since she turned sixty, following an impatient wait for the birthday that would allow her to join the program. Widowed fifteen years and finished with her job of raising her son and daughter and cuddling five grandchildren of her own, she had undergone a radical mastectomy, and the surgery had left her dangerously depressed, "feeling like half a woman."

She lost interest in life. A devout churchgoer, Jennie no longer attended services. Contrary to her habit of careful grooming, she went for days without even combing her hair. Friends worried; when Jennie Forbes didn't even pray any more, they knew she was at her lowest ebb. An aunt told her about the program, and to Jennie it has literally been a godsend.

"You have somebody depending on you again. These kids, their eyes light up when they see me. It's a blessing to have somewhere to *have* to go in the mornings, and it makes a wonderful life for me. Without this I'd have been gone a long time ago. It makes it so that I like my old days better than the young ones. It's made me feel well again even though I'm still sick, because now I have more to give."

She has given unstintingly. Some of the children have stayed in the hospital as long as Jennie has been a foster grandparent, undergoing one operation after another. Some, particularly cancer patients, go home for a while and then come back. When a youngster who has been Jennie's foster grandchild returns to Jackson Memorial, they tell her, "Here's one of your babies back again, Jennie," and she's assigned to the child once more.

Jennie understands as well as anyone the hospital syndrome, that overwhelming fear of being ill, of having one's fate in the hands of other people, of the possibility of never leaving the hospital alive. The fear is tenfold in children who do not understand what is happening and why they have been taken away from their homes and families. Jennie holds them close and croons to them when they are in pain, and when they are feeling better, plays games with them, joins them in solving puzzles, and even teaches them to read.

"They're scared. You got to take their mind from it. When their mamas and daddys aren't there they got only the foster grandparents to hang on to. I take my Bible with me and teach them verses. And I pray with my kids."

There's need for prayer; Jennie feels it gives strength to the little ones who will die before long. The one she remembers most fondly is Theresa, fifteen years old and riddled with cancer. The child was unaware of the hopelessness of her case; Jennie figures that God maybe forgives little white lies.

"When I get well could I come and stay with you?" Theresa asked her. She confided to Jennie that her mother was in prison and that her natural grandmother had taken care of her for a while but no longer wanted her. The child clung to Jennie whose two-hour visits were the high point of the day. Theresa asked nurses not to bathe her, because she wanted to wait for her bath until the afternoon when Jennie would come to her room and do it. Theresa had no clothes except those in which she'd been admitted to the hospital, so Jennie bought her nightgowns and underwear at the dime store so that Theresa could at least have the pleasure of a change.

Jennie herself was twice a patient at the same hospital, undergoing exploratory surgery and then a hysterectomy. She was still weak when she began insisting they wheel her downstairs every day to visit with Theresa, whom she knew was in pain.

During the year she was assigned to Theresa, Jennie cooked food at home and took it to Theresa at the hospital—anything the girl wanted. She ordered fried chicken, collard greens, macaroni and cheese. "I even cooked her chitlins," says Jennie. Her meals were the only ones Theresa ate with pleasure; the chemotherapy treatments affected her for five days afterward, and she refused hospital food. She continued to lose weight; she was smaller by almost half when she was transferred to another hospital, where she died seven weeks later.

Although Jennie's own grandchildren are loved dearly, they are not in her mind nearly as often as her "babies" at Jackson Memorial.

"With some, you take them home and go to bed with them in your mind. Sometimes I can't sleep, and in the morning I have to get cranked up. I think young, and maybe that helps, because once I'm cranked up and ready, I'm *ready*." (An understatement; on the most recent Recognition Day for foster grandparents in the area, Jennie won the disco award for dancing, explaining her talent with, "When the music hits me, I just start to move, that's all.")

Working with the terminally ill has lately become a specialty among professional nurses. Jennie Forbes just does it naturally. "You got to go in that room knowing and believing. I will do everything I can, give these little ones everything I have, knowing they won't be here long."

"Then when they're gone, you see, I can say that I know I made them happy for a little while."

EDITH

In the recreation room of the Los Angeles Juvenile Hall, the faded green walls echoed with the sound of the ping-pong ball as it sped back and forth over the net. The players were an odd couple—a tall black boy of seventeen and, at the other end, her paddle in an expert grip, her iron gray hair flying, a senior citizen backed up to whip the ball in a stinging return. The boy missed, then slammed his paddle on the table in disgust.

"Dammit, grandma, now I can't go home when they let me outta here. I'm the best player in San Fernando—how can I tell them an old woman beat me?"

"Tell them I was once a tournament champion," said the woman.

"Were you? For real?"

Her brown eyes sparkled. "More or less, Frankie. More or less."

Frankie has never forgotten his foster grandmother at Juvenile Hall, and I'll bet none of the other boys "adopted" by Edith Lester have either.

The sort of wisdom needed to be an effective foster

grandparent is not necessarily book learning but rather the knowledge—the moxie, if you will—of having learned through living. At the age of sixty-eight, Edith has both.

For the past seven years she has driven her aging automobile five mornings a week to the sprawling parking lot adjacent to the Los Angeles Juvenile Hall. Inside the grim structure of nondescript stone, behind its barred windows, are always approximately 500 youthful offenders whose average age is fifteen. They are minors who have broken the law in a number of ways—rape, theft, violence, drug involvement, murder—and they are imprisoned at Juvenile Hall while they await trial or sentence or place-ment elsewhere. A few are released to go home.

Edith Lester will not tell you, because she is a woman of delicate manners, that her family in Vienna was one of wealth, erudition, and superb education. She does not dis-cuss it, but it is evident in her face, her speech, her love of music, and in her charity. In Edith's day, the wealthy were brought up to face responsibility for the less fortunate.

What was an elderly lady—an elderly woman of refinement like Edith Lester—doing in a place like Juvenile Hall?

"If I can help only one or two out of a hundred to go straight, I will have done a good job," she says.

Over the years she has befriended and been loved by as many as 5,000 boys and girls. "She don't shine on you," says one. "When grandma Edith talks, you listen. She's telling it to you straight."

Her life has given her almost perfect preparation for being a foster grandparent. Her girlhood in Vienna was marked by her deep devotion to a younger brother who was a victim of Down's syndrome. Edith mothered him, knew his shortcomings and his abilities better than anyone else. She learned that despite his condition he had intelli-gence, and he most certainly had emotions. "He loved me," she says. She returned that love, and it was therefore a sad day when her father arranged for the boy to be taken to an institution, providing funds for his care as long as he lived.

It was probably Edith's affection for this brother that triggered her interest in social work and medicine. But when she told her father she wanted to become a doctor he said, "Nothing doing. We own a department store, and a department store doesn't need a doctor."

Instead of a career in medicine, Edith chose to learn fashion design, but her days off were spent working with asthmatic children.

Edith and her family soon fell under the shadow of Hitler's menace, and Edith was the first out, coming to America to join an aunt. Her parents escaped to Switzerland, but the adored brother was ultimately taken by the Nazis to a concentration camp. A school friend of Edith's who had taught at the institution researched the boy's fate and wrote Edith years later with confirmation that he had been killed.

Despite an unhappy marriage and an extremely successful career as a fashion designer (in America she became the favorite "ghost" of the famous couturier Don Loper), Edith continued to indulge her faculty for nurturing others. While her son was away at college, she took a nursing course that would permit her to instruct exceptional children. When her divorce necessitated higher earnings than she received for teaching the retarded, she went back to designing. By that time she was in the grip of arthritis, which prevented her being on her feet all day, "running around the tables to cut with heavy scissors," and so at fifty-nine Edith went on disability.

At home in her tiny Los Angeles apartment she saw a television program about the Foster Grandparent Plan, and a light went on in her head. "That is what I want to do," Edith Lester told herself.

Her income was low enough for admission, and she joined the program on her sixtieth birthday, telling the director she would like to be assigned to Juvenile Hall.

"Why there?" asked the director. "You've had so much experience with retarded children."

"Because I know that in working with the retarded," said Edith, "only a very few can benefit from my help, and those I can only make a little happy. But the children in trouble with the law—if I can convince them to turn their backs on crime, that we need then as good citizens . . ."

"These kids are tough," said the director. "Aren't you afraid?"

"No," said Edith Lester.

Although Edith's entire story is remarkable, I think her lack of fear impresses me the most. I have visited a correctional facility only once—the Fred C. Nelles school for delinquent boys in Whittier, California. When I walked into a room full of boys, there was dead silence. They merely stared at me until a freckle-faced boy of about sixteen asked if he could have my autograph. That broke the ice, and they crowded around me, handing me scraps of paper and pencils, wanting to have their pictures taken with me.

One boy told me he hadn't thought I'd come or that if I did, I'd be surrounded by police. When I told him such a thing hadn't occurred to me he said, "You mean you trust us?"

I said that of course I did, and later I heard a whisper going around the room; they were passing the word, "She says she trusts us."

On the way out of the building the head of the school asked me if I had any idea what those boys were there for.

"No," I said. "They all look like the boy next door."

The man shook his head. "Mrs. Reagan, they are here because they have committed armed robbery and rape and murder."

A chill ran down my spine at that moment, at my naïveté, but what remained with me was their interest— pride, I suppose I should say—in the fact that I trusted them.

Edith Lester has always known how important that is to these kids in trouble with the law. She began work at Juvenile Hall without fear and says now, "The children and I, we have had a seven-year love affair."

She originally intended working with the girls, hoping to teach them to sew, perhaps interest them in fashion design; or, at the very least, teach them to sew on buttons, how to mend; give them an interest in grooming themselves. She had it all figured out that she'd do for them the same thing she'd done with the mentally retarded girls she had taught so many years before. She would test them and recommend to those with enough ability that they learn how to use power sewing machines so they could find work in factories. But there weren't that many girls, and besides, there was already a foster grandmother working with them. But there were a great many boys, and she'd had a son of her own, and so Edith went to work with the boys in bungalows C and D.

There were forty every day, twenty in each bungalow, a changing parade of boys who were all hers, because Edith was their only foster grandparent. They were first offenders, those who could get along without fighting, less dangerous than the homicidal inmates locked alone in their rooms behind one-way windows.

The bungalows were on the very end of the central heating system so that during the winter they were bitterly cold and terribly hot in summer. The discomfort didn't deter Edith from going to work a half hour early every morning. She wanted that time to talk to the kids before classes started. And of course there were always the newcomers, as well as the children waiting to go to court or the dentist.

Each morning she went directly to the day room, where the kids would chorus, "Good morning grandma. How are you today?" If they didn't greet her when they returned after classes, she would tease them, "What's this?

No hi, no nothing?" Then they'd troop up to her, mending their manners. Over the years dozens of boys said to her, "You know, grandma, you give us a chance to be gentlemen."

They weren't, of course. They came from backgrounds that made them as hard as steel. Their stories were so sad, so hopeless and horrible that Edith determined she would never take her work home with her. She couldn't have endured twenty-four-hours-a-day empathy for these boys she calls bruised children. She made it a practice to block it all from her mind each time she drove home. She made herself forget their names and told them not to feel rejected because of it, because she never forgot a face and would remember them that way, always.

They came from homes where the father was repeatedly sent to jail, and when he got out on parole he came home to make his wife pregnant again. He paid no attention to his children; they didn't know him. One boy's father was in jail for fifteen years, and there were fourteen children in the house. Another had a mother who was a prostitute, and he was shoved from one foster home to another and had no one to turn to. There were incest cases—yes, the boys, too. Parents drank and vented their drunkenness on their children, and some of the children became drunkards themselves.

When the boys left Juvenile Hall to go home or to another placement, they would hug Edith goodbye and say, "Grandma, I won't see you again, because I won't be back here. I promise." Those who did return, having broken the law once more, hung their heads in shame when they saw her. "I tried so hard, grandma, I did, but I couldn't help it. You don't know what it means to live in the ghetto."

She understood. They were caught in their old environment with no other place to go. If they had belonged to a gang, they had to return to it. To refuse could mean they would be knifed; very few Mexican boys living in East

Los Angeles found it possible to stay away from the gang life.

The professional staff at Juvenile Hall gave Edith Lester a free hand to do as she wished. She was the only one who could counsel the children, because she was the only one who had the time to listen to them. She is a past master at listening and knows it is perhaps the most important thing a foster grandparent can do.

"It goes both ways," she says. "I've learned from them too. I learned about a kind of life that I couldn't have imagined. They tell me their miseries, and I've told them some of mine."

She became such a good listener, so attuned to the boys, that she knew instinctively when they were telling the truth and when they were lying. She trusted them so completely that she looked at their records, which were always available to her, only if she doubted the tales they told her. As Edith herself puts it, "I knew whether they were up front or giving me a b.s. story."

From her this seems an uncharacteristic use of street language, and when it is remarked upon, she smiles and says, "I am not altogether a sweet person, you understand. I like clean fun I can joke about on a level they understand, and somehow they appreciate this more than if I said things like 'Yes, my dear' and 'No, my dear.' Then I would be shining on them, and they would know it."

While she uses the vernacular and their slang, Edith of course eschews all foul language, and the boys are fiercely protective of her in this regard. Upon entering a room she has often heard one of them say, "Watch your language—here comes grandma." The counselors themselves often use gutter talk, and when they failed to clean up their speech within Edith's earshot, the boys were outraged.

They worried, too, that she might not be safe in her own world. "It's rough out there, grandma. You take care. Come back here healthy tomorrow."

44

When she told them of the mugging attempt, they were furious. Edith had taken two women, one blind and one in her nineties, to a lecture that ended at eleven P.M. As they left the theater, Edith told them to stand outside while she got her car from the parking lot behind the building. Walking alone on the dark street, she suddenly felt someone tugging at her purse. With her free hand she grabbed the boy's hair and didn't let go even when a second boy jabbed her in the ribs. It was a dual attack designed to make the victim release her purse. Not Edith. She yanked at the kid's hair and yelled, "You just wait, buster, until I catch up with you at Juvenile Hall!" Whereupon the muggers fled, and Edith still had her purse.

It is typical of her that when she told the story at the hall the next morning, she added the fact she'd been grateful to still have her car keys. "Otherwise, I wouldn't have been able to face those two old women waiting for me to drive them home."

Twenty grandsons had other thoughts. "Did you get a good look at the creeps?" they wanted to know. "When those dirtbags get in here, you just nail them for us!"

"I appreciate your concern," said Edith. "But let me point something out to you. You are upset about this experience because you know me. But if you had been outside yourselves and you didn't know me and you saw me on a dark street, you'd have tried to mug me, too. Right?"

They nodded agreement.

"So next time, *think* about what you are doing." Her talk is straight, and they know it. When approaching the newcomers, she asked their names and about their family life. Few objected to her questioning. Occasionally, a black boy would freeze, but Edith understood it was because he had never been spoken to by an adult white woman, and he was shy. Once the initial talk was over with, this one-to-one chat, the newly arrived merged with the group, and Edith found she could handle all twenty when left alone with them in the bungalow. Never once was there an incidence of even minor violence.

She later worked with the tougher criminals, but even when her charges were mere runaways or incorrigibles, some would confess serious crimes to her. Including attempts at murder. They gave her back her trust.

She probed for their hobbies. If she learned that a boy had a talent, sketching for example, she tried to interest him in applying to a school that would further his ability.

She gave them her own idea of how to get a job. "Don't waste your time filling out applications at personnel departments of large corporations. Believe me, they get stuck into a file and are never taken out. Instead, I suggest you go to the small shops in your neighborhood. To food stores, watch repair shops, restaurants, shoemakers. Introduce yourself and tell them you could be there every day after school, that you're willing to work for nothing if you can learn a trade or a business."

She explained to them the system of apprenticeship in Europe, the years of work for so very little, but in the end having a craft, a skill. The idea made sense to many who used it to advantage when they were released from Juvenile Hall. She would see them on the street, in traffic sometimes, and they would call to her, "Hi, grandma! I'm doing great! Thank you!"

To some of the boys, she has spoken of foreign lands, of cultures, of history, and often of our own government. The last because so few had any idea of the workings of our democracy. Many hadn't even the dimmest idea of what a mayor or governor does, let alone the Constitution or the Bill of Rights.

She has doted on the boys of higher intelligence, amazed to find so many who have been fascinated to learn how to play chess. She insists that some have beaten her in as few as three moves. Edith is fond of chess because it is a game of skill rather than luck, and she's as good at it as she is at ping-pong. (She *was* a tournament champion.)

She taught them math, and when she found a child who allowed that he liked arithmetic, she asked if he knew what math stands for. "A clear thinker. If you know math then you are able to think clearly about life. That's what you know as common sense. Do you know what logic means? Let me explain." And she'd be off, hoping to strike a spark in the intelligence of the boy.

She taught them English, her second language—which Edith Lester speaks more correctly than a great many native Americans. She is fussy about language, deeply aware that without precise communication it is difficult to stay out of trouble and most certainly difficult to become successful. A purist, she is horrified when the boys use filthy words in place of object, subject, verb, adjective. Four out of five words from the mouths of the inmates are vulgarities, and Edith has warned them that few people in the decent world would be able to understand what they were attempting to say. They had better, she said, clean out their mouths and learn respect for the English language.

For the older children she obtained a booklet of tests used for high-school graduation and worked with them to prepare them for the exams. From the automobile club she collected maps of cities and showed them where they lived, other countries, and where she had traveled. She has tried to give them the world.

She taught them what she could about clothes merely by being unfailingly well groomed. She knew she could not teach the matter of taste, because her own could never be instilled in youngsters who love wild colors and hold dear their own ideas of what constitutes a status symbol in wardrobe. But they did notice Edith's clothes, made on her sewing machine at home, never loud, always in quiet good taste, and they would say to each other, "Our grandmother always looks nice."

She taught them how to waltz. The dance was something they'd never heard of, let alone the music. Edith's Viennese ears had suffered through hours of what she calls their drug music, because she was too polite to object to it. But one day in the lunchroom she began to sing a Strauss tune and grabbed a tall boy away from his spaghetti to whirl him around the room. One, two, three, one, two, three. After that, they all wanted to learn how to waltz.

Edith has taught them decency. A young black who called her Grandma Dynamo told her he was a pimp for five girls.

"Which one are you going to marry?" she asked him, setting him up. He was horrified, of course.

"Who, me? Are you kidding? I wouldn't marry any of them. *I* have to marry a nice girl."

Edith landed on him with both feet. How come he could contribute to the ruin of the lives of these girls and yet think he was deserving of a girl who was beyond reproach? "What you are doing is not very nice. It's bad enough that a girl hasn't more respect for her own body, but for you to make money from this is terrible. If you want a decent girl, then go out and make a decent living."

It made sense to the boy, or seemed to, because he began coming to her often for more advice.

She taught them hope. And ambition. When a boy of intelligence was depressed, she would tell him of his own worth. "You have a good mind. Go out and get an education. Education is where it all begins. We need people like you to get us a higher standard of living, a better culture. If you don't care, then it is the uneducated ones who will take over. You are our future."

Edith comes close to blushing when she tells of the day she had to teach a boy about sex. "Imagine! I, who had never discussed the subject with my women friends—who was embarrassed to speak of it with my own son! And here was this boy. He was no older than fourteen, and one day he asked to be excused from class because he wanted to talk with me about something that was bothering him.

"He told me that he had made a girl pregnant. And

then that he'd also made her girlfriend pregnant. When the mother of the second girl found out about it, she had beaten him up. He'd been so furious about it that he'd thrown a bomb into the woman's house. And that's why he was in Juvenile Hall.

"What did this Lothario want to talk to me about? He asked me what sexual intercourse is. He wanted to know what is it that people call a climax. He wanted to know the names of things, verbs and nouns. So there I was, explaining all this to a boy child who was a stranger to me. It was most embarrassing, but I had to do it, of course. He had such confidence in me."

Edith remembers "a beautiful blond boy who looked like a little angel." He was the son of a psychiatrist and an actress and lived with his parents in an elite neighborhood. Edith surmised he was in Juvenile Hall because he was neglected. According to law officers, it was because he had wrecked his mother's car. He came back a second time for smashing another car. The boy was often sent expensive candy, perhaps by his parents, and whenever he opened a box he passed it around to the other children, every one of whom during that period was either black or Chicano. Such a generous gesture had been unknown to them, and they accepted him as one of them. The blond boy was grateful. He told Edith, "I've always gone to private schools, to military schools. This is the best school I've ever known. These guys teach me more about life than anyone else can." Edith Lester could understand that.

She was never able to learn how she might help the drug addicts. This was the realm of doctors, and unfortunately, Edith had never earned the medical degree she had so earnestly wanted. So she told the addicts the same thing she had told her own son when he first went away to college: "You must always be your own master, no matter what you are doing. If you mess up with drugs or booze you will be less than an animal. Because you have destroyed basic instinct, and an animal never loses that. It is up to you—whatever you want to make of yourself."

If Edith has a philosophy, it is the effort to make the world a better place than when she entered it. She is most certainly doing a good job of it, and she is thriving. It's a philosophy she taught her son, who will marry shortly and so gives Edith hope for a grandchild of her own flesh and blood. Her son recently told her, "Mom, you must never stop working. When *you* stop working, your wits will go away."

So Edith keeps on. On weekdays she nurtures the unfortunate children and says, "They are my life, those kids."

In her free time she creates lovely things at her sewing machine while listening to classical music. She attends concerts and walks among the camellias in Descanso Gardens. If and when she has the money for extra gasoline, she picks up a few octogenarians from nursing homes and takes "the old ladies" for a drive.

"It isn't right," says Edith Lester, "to allow those old people to vegetate."

DOT

In her lifetime, Dorothy Fife has had two husbands, two sons, and too much alcohol. Her early life gives us no reason for the crutch of heavy drinking. Dot grew up under the big sky of Montana in a happy family living in a small town. At the time she first married, she had never been more than fifty miles away from home.

The first marriage was not a good one, but it was nothing drastic enough to turn Dot to drinking. She began slowly, taking an occasional drink to "go along with the crowd." At the time of her second marriage, she still disliked the taste of liquor, but this husband drank quite a bit, and Dot joined him. When he became ill, she used the pressure as an excuse, and it wasn't long before she was drinking too much at night and taking a nip or two in the morning. Leaning on it, she became a slave to it. Dot was simply a victim of a body chemistry that creates a person who will become addicted to alcohol—if that person ever begins social drinking.

Like most alcoholics, she did not recognize her sickness until she had gone through many hellish years. Together with her husband she failed in attempts to control the drinking. When her husband died in 1969, Dot was fifty-four years old, filled with grief, and more dependent than ever on the bottle. Loneliness was a new excuse. There were friends in St. Anthony, Idaho, where she had moved with her husband when he was transferred there by the Forest Service. But even those friends were slipping away, disgusted with Dot's habit.

That first year of widowhood was the worst of her life. Three times she was admitted to hospitals, ostensibly for one ailment or another but in truth to "dry out." Typical of the alcoholic, and unbelievable as it is to others, Dot did not know, or refused to recognize, the source of her physical problems.

That changed when she joined Alcoholics Anonymous, a move she says has literally saved her life. And the past dozen years have been the best of all. She was working at a gas station in St. Anthony when her sister told her about the Foster Grandparent Program. Dot had been bored with her job for some time, and her sons, who through the years had understood her illness and remained supportive, disagreed when she considered returning to her previous work as a beautician. She should try to find something else to do, they said.

In trepidation she went to apply at the FGP in Blackfoot, Idaho, afraid they would not accept her because she was an alcoholic. People don't always understand that alcoholism is involuntary and that those who join AA are almost certain to stay away from liquor for the rest of their lives. She needn't have worried, because when she stated she was a member of AA the interviewer didn't turn a hair. Dot was hired on the spot.

"We'll put you in the State Youth Service Center in St. Anthony. You'll be assigned to a girls' cottage there and have two granddaughters."

St. Anthony's facility is a last-ditch institution. In effect it is a juvenile jail, and its unwilling residents range in age from nine to seventeen. They are hard-core cases; by the time they are sent to St. Anthony's, they are in real trouble. One of the six cottages is maximum security and within its walls is a lot of violence. "These kids don't get sent to St. Anthony's for doing nothing, for going to Sunday School," says Dot.

Many residents have been in a traditional jail for perhaps a month, awaiting sentence, and they would arrive at St. Anthony's in relatively healthy condition. But the others arrived under the influence of drugs or alcohol.

When fourteen-year-old Lucy arrived, she was so drunk she couldn't stand upright. By the time she dried out, she was able to recognize that she'd been "given" a grandmother, a pleasant woman who spent a couple of hours with her every weekday, sewing, playing cards. The fact didn't make Lucy feel any happier about having been put into St. Anthony's. From a solid upper-middle-class family, Lucy loathed her incarceration in "the pit" and fumed against authority. Things turned brighter for her only on the day when, over a game of double solitaire, grandma Dot said, "Lucy, did you ever get so drunk you thought it'd be smart to go out and break some windows?"

Lucy stared at her. "How'd you know that?"

"I've thought of it myself when I was drunk. Even did it one time, matter of fact."

"You got drunk?"

"Sure. All the time, back then. I used to have to have a drink first thing when I got out of bed. But I don't drink any more. I'm an alcoholic, Lucy."

"Holy gee!" said Lucy. She was so impressed that she turned their conversation to the subject of drinking every morning, and Dot talked about it, freely and truthfully.

"I might as well have been three years old most of my adult life," she told the girl. "Because when you're an alcoholic you're nothing but a three-year-old. Not good for much—except maybe to need people to take care of you."

Lucy listened, by now convinced this elderly woman was no threat to her but perhaps even a friend, and she began to open up, telling Dot of her own dependence on alcohol. Eavesdropping on their conversation one morning was twelve-year-old Sandra who sat in a corner listening to every word. Dot was aware of this but ignored her until Sandra joined her and Lucy and said she was interested.

It became a foursome when fourteen-year-old Laura began sitting with them. Laura had never known her father, and her mother, a hopeless drug addict, had begun shooting Laura up with dope when the child was six. That was how Laura got started.

Almost 200 youths, both girls and boys, were confined on the "campus," and according to an administrator, 99 percent of them had drug and/or alcohol problems, often attempting to smuggle dope and liquor past security. As many as 85 percent of the kids came from homes where the parents also were involved with drugs; yet for all these youngsters only one counselor was provided by the center to deal with the subject of drugs.

Dot soon found herself with a daily group at her feet, Socrates style. She worried, therefore, that she was breaking the by-laws of the Foster Grandparent Program, which allows only two children a day to each grandparent. To rectify the situation, she offered to work with the kids on her own time and was soon putting in six hours a day.

Then the boys discovered Grandma Dot, seeing her in the halls or cafeteria and asking when they could talk with her. Soon she offered two meetings or classes each day. Attendance was optional, yet there were usually between five and fifteen girls, and the boy's group grew to more than twenty.

Dot didn't begin working with the boys until she had succeeded in bringing the AA organization *to* the center. Working only with the girls had become too heavy a burden for her; after listening to full-fledged alcoholics between the ages of nine and eighteen—the things they had done and were ashamed of, the things that had been done to them, all the hurt they were holding inside—Dot would go home "wrung out like a rag." But she knew this was what they needed, the opportunity to let it all pour out with the knowledge that not a word of it would be repeated.

And so, within four years, Dot had engineered the involvement of the AA within the St. Anthony Center. This gave her more time with the children and more time for relaxation, but most importantly, it provided follow-up help for the youngsters who left the center. AA members throughout the state of Idaho contact children immediately upon their release to offer them continued support.

"That's when they are the most scared," says Dot. "When they go back out and have to keep away from alcohol."

Additionally, those children at the center who had pleaded with Dot to help their alcoholic parents were now involved in Alateen, the AA program for those who must live with alcoholics and which uses the same program as AA.

"If you live with an alcoholic long enough," says Dot, "you're as sick as they are, and you need help. AA combines the program to include all drugs—after all, alcohol itself is a drug. AA deals with the mental, physical, and spiritual aspects, healing in all three areas."

Once she had time to include boys in her meetings, Dot was in seventh heaven. She began giving a party once a month for them all, with coffee and cookies. "I love kids," she says. "I collect kids."

She took time for a college course devoted to the study of drugs and their effects, but in the long run she learned more about drugs from the young people at the center than she did from books.

And she taught them. She told them that joining AA was completely up to them, that they had to help themselves. "You can do anything you want with your life. It's your choice."

She told them that alcoholics are never successful in rescuing their own lives until they admit they have a drinking problem. Until then they will steal, injure people, do all manner of things they'd never consider doing while sober. "These are things that booze, and drugs, make you do. Your mood changes, you're out of control, you live by impulse. Every one of you thinks you're unique, that no one else has the problems you do. But in truth you're all the same. Now you take me, for instance. About ten years ago . . ." And she'd be off, telling them of something idiotic, or dangerous, she had done while under the influence of alcohol.

The most difficult thing for Dot has been getting them to admit to others and to themselves that they have a problem, and it is a joy to watch the release when this finally happens. It is often accompanied by a flood of tears, a weeping for happiness that it will no longer be necessary to lie to the world and to themselves. "Some will get up and say 'I am an alcoholic' just to be smart," says Dot. "But you can tell the difference. When it really happens, it's beautiful to see."

One girl resisted admitting her problem throughout several years and a half dozen trips to St. Anthony's but has since joined AA and rounded up several new members. Dot has had scores of such triumphs. Lucy still belongs to AA, has married, and has a baby. Sandra also is married, is a mother—and is still dry. So is Laura.

They and many others write Grandma Dot, whom they remember as their "swinging grandmother." The reputation began when they learned she bowls and plays golf, but once they taught her to disco, the appellation caught on for good.

She hears from great batches of kids, all of whom have stuck with their vows to quit both drugs and alcohol. It's the ones she does not hear from that she still worries about. "I have to separate them from the others, block them from my mind. They're gone now, after all, and all I can do is pray for them. Maybe He listens to me—I do feel that my landing in the Foster Grandparent Program was an act of God."

So there it is—supply for the demand. These children needed somebody who could understand and who could help. And who better than Dot Fife?

DOMINICK

The gymnasium in the correctional school for boys near Cleveland is as big and cavernous as most gyms; the difference is that its doors are locked. All of them, always. The minors incarcerated in that building have committed serious crimes—an example is the boy who is there for having murdered an old man in a nearby city—and the authorities take no chances that any might escape. The atmosphere within the facility is tough and tight, and violence among the boys is not unusual.

In the gym, however, for four hours each weekday, there is a lighthearted air, the big room ringing with shouts and laughter. An incredible scene is played out there when foster grandparent Dominick Sylvester holds sway with his "class."

The boys show up in shorts, some also in T-shirts, some in bare feet, some in well-worn athletic shoes. A staff member locks the door behind them, then opens a door leading to the stockroom from which the youths drag mats and place them in a long line on the gymnasium floor.

"Thank you, boys," says Dominick who believes in

teaching courtesy and respect along with his forte of acrobatics. ("How are they ever going to learn to thank people
if you don't thank them? You can't treat them like something to kick around and then expect them to be decent to
others.") Dominick is seventy-four years old, a short man
of slight build, with the fair complexion of his mother
whose people came from northern Italy "where you can
walk into Switzerland."

Any one of the hulking boys would make two of Dom
Sylvester, yet when he is in command, they toe the line
with a respect that is apparent in the glow with which they
watch him. They do his bidding, and Dom's orders are not
easy to follow. "Do a back handspring." Or, "Let's try a
cartwheel ending in a side somersault."

They respect him because he himself does these
things. Well, not the latter; that's something Dominick *used*
to do, but advancing years have made it impossible for
him. The boys tease him, "You only think you're getting
old, pops." But he can teach them everything, because
when he could still do the stunts, he taught boys who have
taught other boys—back through the three years Dom has
been a foster grandfather. There's always someone there
who can illustrate by example.

It is impossible to believe Dominick's seventy-four
years when he puts himself at the head of a line of boys,
and suddenly the old man becomes a zephyr, a small whirling circle as his body turns swiftly down the line of mats in
a forward roll. The boys follow in a rolling line, each a few
feet behind the other, some bumbling slightly, some almost as graceful as Dominick.

It is the warmup for the class, during which they will
learn gymnastics and tumbling. They will practice handstands, headstands, backward and forward handsprings,
hand balancing. When it is something dangerous, such as a
back handspring, Dominick ties a safety belt around the
youth's waist, which is then held by boys standing on

either side of the mat, and they can tighten their hold and thus break a fall.

Second only to Dominick's affection for "his boys" is the old man's love of show business. It is a fever contracted in his extreme youth, and he grins as he admits it has never left him. In a way, teaching the youths at the Cuyahoga Hills Boys School is the closest he can come to the stage today, because it's to be hoped some of these kids will be able to build careers out of the talents given them by Dominick.

"Not Olympics," says Dominick. "I don't believe in working that hard, a dedication of a whole lifetime. There are so many other things in life. For these kids, I think gymnastics are good for two reasons—it gives them confidence in themselves, and it teaches self-discipline. Maybe, when they get out of here, these two things will give them what it takes to make it on their own and stay our of jail for the rest of their lives."

Self-discipline is something Dom knows a lot about. He and his six brothers and three sisters learned it from their father, a man so in thrall to acrobatics that he hung rings and bars from the bedroom ceiling and took each son from the cradle to teach him tricks before he could walk.

As a boy himself, Dominick's father had turned back somersaults from the rear end of a moving wagon, and he never ceased his love of tumbling. He earned the family's living as an electrician; as a hobby, he created things in silver so beautiful that several were placed in museums, and he saw to it that each of his children played at least one musical instrument. But gymnastics were his passion. From the neighborhood he collected old mattresses to use as mats for the kids, and by the time Dominick was ten years old, he and two of his brothers were remarkable in their section of Cleveland because the trio would some-times interrupt their walk on a city street by doing a kick-over back somersault in unison and then blithely continue on their way.

These were the two brothers who joined Dom in the gym every afternoon after school. They put together an act, hand balancing, etc., and soon were working shows in local movie houses and auditoriums. Dominick was so good that he attracted the attention of a professional from Chicago who saw Dom working out in a gym.

"Have you ever done a handstand on a person?" the stranger asked.

When Dominick said no, the man lay supine on the floor and picked him up and held him, and Dom pressed into a handstand as though he'd done it all his life. Then and there the man wanted Dom to join him in an act on the Orpheum circuit, but the boy was seventeen, and his parents said no. The acrobatics were hard enough on his mother who often had to turn her eyes away from the unnerving sight of her offspring leaping and flipping and whirling around the house and back yard.

So Dominick settled for work as an acrobatic clown in the one-ring Elk circus when it came to the area. It was small-time show business, but it was show business, and he loved it. At twenty, Dom teamed up with a tap dancer he'd met at the Palace theater. The dancer was strong enough to "pitch" Dom and taught him enough steps so that Dominick could combine tap with his acrobatics and keep time to the music. His partner worked the Keith circuit, which was roughly between Chicago and New York, but as a team they stayed close to Cleveland. "If I'd ignored my parents," Dom says, "maybe I could have gone places in vaudeville, but they wanted me to stay with the family, and so I did."

None of Dom's pleasure in his work would have been possible without his father's discipline, a factor in Dominick's life as far back as he could remember. One day the young Dominick brought home a hammer he had found.

"Where did you get it?" his father asked.

"On that dirt road up north. There wasn't anybody around, and the hammer was in the middle of the road."

"Take it back. It still belongs to somebody. Put it where you found it."

On another day Dominick was sent to the store for bread and on the way stopped to talk with a friend. "My father passed us just as this kid said a bad word, and dad heard it," Dominick recalls. "I didn't say it, but he heard me talking with a kid that did, and so I was punished when I got home."

This seems harsh contrasted with today's permissive ways in rearing children, yet all these years later Dom Sylvester says, "We all loved our father very much. We still miss him."

There was no grass in the Sylvester back yard. Any grass that tried to grow was trampled by the troops of aspiring gymnasts working out there every day. When they were afraid to try new stunts, their father would show them how and then tell them, "I know you can do it. Now *you* must know you can do it. So—do it." He played with them like a brother, but he only had to say something once; his children obeyed him.

Dominick uses the same philosophy and tactics with his boys in the gym, and it is said that in many tight situations Dominick is the only one the boys will listen to. He is pleased by this because he had tried for more than a year to get a job at the school. "I wanted to get in here and teach these boys and maybe turn their lives around. When my wife quit work, our lowered income qualified me for the foster grandparents, and so I got started. I've told some of the boys they could make a career of it—I've even teamed up some of them. Some have been interested in joining a circus or carnival. *Any*thing is better than them getting back into the streets and ending up here again."

Abrams is one boy with potential. He wanted to learn to tap dance, and Dom taught him a few steps, along with the advice to keep practicing. "Your feet are clumsy when you start. You've got to keep at it."

Dominick pounds at the importance of practice. "You've got to do it every day, every other day at a minimum. You lose it if you don't—look what happened to me. You've got to concentrate, do it with all your body, altogether with a lot of whip, real fast. I'd show you, but I can't do it any more. Harley, get over here and show Scott how to do it."

Prior to joining the FGP, Dominick had not practiced sufficiently to stay in good condition. In his later years he never dreamed he'd be called upon to once again be a gymnast, so with the advent of the FGP he had to work hard. He "got back" to doing a front handspring and not long go, finally, handstands.

"The first time I tried handstands again I was in my sixties. I went down in the basement of our home and tried to kick my feet up to the wall. For a couple of weeks I didn't have the power or the push to get my feet even halfway up. The day I touched them to the wall, I let myself come down and then got on my knees and made the sign of the cross and thanked the Lord, because I figured I was going to be able to do a handstand again."

His teaching effects wonderful things. Stanley is a squarely built lad with a simian gait who, when he first took lessons from Dominick, "always fell to the floor like a sack of potatoes." Today he is a model of grace and precision, and Dom says that even the boy's posture has changed for the better.

For a long time Enrico ignored Dominick's advice about practice. Enrico wanted to do handstands, and Dom showed him how and said, "If you want to do that stuff, practice the way I tell you. If you do it your way, you'll never get it." Enrico finally listened, worked, and became so adept be could walk up and down steps on his hands. "He could even jump from step to step," says Dominick proudly.

Dom's daily four hours are divided into three classes,

with short breaks between, and his pleasure compounds as each boy enters the gym. They get an earful of philosophy along with their acrobatics. Dom tells them they don't have to be millionaires to live happily in this world. "When you leave here you can learn how to get along on very little. Crime is going to get you no place but here, and maybe, when you're older, a worse place."

He's rather sure he has been instrumental in straightening out, in time, many young men. Last spring a boy who was to graduate from the school in June made a trip with a social worker to apply to a college. When Jon came back, he looked up Dominick right away to tell him about the great gym at the college. "Jon will make it, I know," says Dominick. "Because when he started to learn how to roll, he stuck with it. The others would start a basketball game, but not Jon. He practiced the whole hour, and that means this boy will get whatever he goes after."

Dom is justly proud of his own children, a daughter who is an attorney and a son who has a Ph.D. in engineering, but the biggest smile to cross his face comes when he finishes a session with the boys in the gym and says, "I really love these kids!"

HELEN

S heila was three years old when her mother abandoned
her to a hospital in Tallahassee, Florida and thirteen
years old before Helen Heffernan took her on as a foster
grandchild.

In the intervening ten years, Sheila lived in a world
impossible to imagine. A victim of congenital rubella as a
result of her mother's bout with measles during the preg-
nancy, Sheila was blind, she was deaf, she was autistic,
she had an abnormally small brain. At thirteen she still
functioned mentally at the level of a six- to nine-month-old
baby. By comparison, Helen Keller was a fortunate being.

Those in the medical profession had given up on Sheila's case; it was hopeless, they said. So hopeless—and so
unbearable for the child—that not infrequently she was the
subject of studies by postgraduate students at nearby
Florida State University. The students, many of them serving internships for medical careers, observed Sheila's self-
destructive behavior; the way she constantly injured
herself, not only jabbing fingers into her ears and eyes but
insistently beating her head against anything she could

find, most particularly sharp edges. She was an unusual case, and they viewed her as a challenge, inventing ways to discourage her from inflicting injury on herself.

And then they bumped into Sheila's newly assigned foster grandmother who did not always approve or agree with the treatment of the child—and said as much.

Helen Heffernan had had only one foster grandchild prior to Sheila, a little girl born without kneecaps, who achieved locomotion by crawling on the floor. Her tantrums were violent until Helen offered her the love that works so unfailingly in the Foster Grandparent Program. Christy improved so dramatically her mother took her home.

Then Helen learned about Sheila, and when she inquired if she might be assigned to her, she was told not to bother with the child. "She's been hopeless for years," they said. "You'll never be able to improve her behavior. We've given up on her."

"Not me," said Helen. "I'm at least going to try."

Sheila had always worn a helmet to prevent damage to her head, yet within only three months Helen could remove the helmet without worry when she took Sheila outdoors. There she would push the girl back and forth on a swing, and for a half hour the child would cease hitting herself. But Helen suspected that Sheila *wanted* to inflict pain. When Helen placed her arm so that it interfered with Sheila's attempt to hit her own head, the girl would push Helen's arm away. And slowly Helen began to realize that there was pleasure that accompanied the pain, that the injuries were something that Sheila needed to inflict on herself. The question was why, and there was no answer. The only hope for the child was to minimize the self-mutilation.

Helen tried to keep the girl's hands busy; she bought her a soft toy Sheila liked to fondle, but the attention span was never longer than three minutes. Helen spent hours holding and rocking the child, treating her like a baby because, with the mentality of an infant, that's precisely what Sheila was.

Realizing the love and affection were helping, Helen wanted a way to identify herself to Sheila so that the child could differentiate between her foster grandmother and the three shifts of nursing staff. She solved this by rubbing baby oil on her arm, and when she arrived each morning she held her arm beneath Sheila's nose. Before long, whenever Helen came near the child, Sheila would reach up and grab her arm. Helen talked to her, putting her mouth near the bone in back of the girl's ear. "Grandma loves you, Sheila. You are my baby." To some, this attempt at communication with a deaf child may seem utterly worthless, yet Sheila responded by making sounds. Helen beamed and told the staff, "She's talking back to me."

She made notes, a regular log, of Sheila's responses, keeping track of everything that happened during the daily two hours she spent with the youngster, and these were used more than once by medical students as research for their term papers.

Meanwhile, Helen was doing her own homework. She read everything she could find on the subject of autistic children, those who seem to be off in a world of their own and never communicate with reality. She sent as far away as England for material on retardation. She wrote to Washington asking for information regarding mental illness. And later, she wrote me, her letter filled with enthusiasm about the program and the good things that were happening within it at Tallahassee. I remember that she expressed quite strongly her support for both my husband and myself, in particular my efforts in behalf of the Foster Grandparent Program.

Apparently Helen Heffernan seldom does anything in a halfhearted way. She doesn't know what half a heart is. I mentioned earlier that the university students "bumped into" Helen, and they did indeed, colliding with a woman unafraid to voice her opinion.

In working with a severe case, such as Sheila's, something called "adverse therapy" is used. In simple language this means finding ways to help a patient cease self-destructive behavior. The ways often seem cruel, and in a sense they are, but they are last-resort treatments with the humane goal of saving the patient. Helen attended some of these adverse-therapy classes and watched as each student, many on assignment for internship, tried his or her own idea. She stiffened in horror when they squirted water into Sheila's ears, blew a hair dryer into her face. They shone a flashlight into the child's eyes and wrote in their notes that Sheila responded. Helen disagreed. When Helen returned from a two-week vacation, Sheila had acquired new behavior patterns very probably initiated through recent adverse therapy. One was sliding beneath a bed sheet and staying there, a habit Sheila has retained.

Helen fought these treatments every step of the way. "I am not a professional like you people," she said, "but I have enough motherly instinct to know these actions are not appropriate. They will not be effective."

The students paid no attention to the seventy-three-year-old woman who persisted in collaring any who would listen to her.

"I think Sheila is banging her head as a way of communicating," she said. "She is trying to tell somebody something of what is going on inside herself."

Helen was so empathic with the suffering of Sheila that she went so far as to question the possibility of a lobotomy—"anything to stop this awful turmoil inside of her"—even if it meant destroying a portion of the brain.

She noted the fact of Sheila's many and continuing illnesses—diverticulitis, severe ear infections, a hernia —and one day she said to a future psychiatrist, "Sheila's behavior has a lot to do with pain. We can't separate pain from the way she acts."

"Mrs. Heffernan," he said, "we are not interested in any of the nursing aspects of the case. . . ."

Helen's eyes were suddenly filled with sparks. "Well, I *am!*" she said.

Whatever it is that has taken hold—"the nursing part," Helen's love, her innate common sense—her way with Sheila has worked miracles. The child is now seventeen years old, fully grown ("My Sheila has a beautiful body"), and after three years under Helen's care has markedly ceased harming herself. When she puts her arms around Helen's neck, the foster grandmother beams. "You see, she loves me."

Helen doesn't know if Sheila's mental level has increased during their years together. "They don't tell the foster grandparents about things like mental tests," says Helen, her subtle wink hinting she'd very much like to know such results. "Let's just say it's enough for me to know that her self-destruction has lessened so dramatically. After all, she'd been termed hopeless." With an obvious wink this time, she says, "I'm a firecracker with these kids."

The fact is well known by assorted staff members to whom Helen Heffernan's skills have been apparent for some time. She regularly attended the team meetings, the rehabilitation meetings, and spoke candidly about her opinions of what worked and what did not. Many times her ideas were against the main thrust of what everyone else was attempting, but in many cases the others had already exhausted their own efforts, and in the long run they listened to Helen.

No one else in the Tallahassee program has had as much success; her batting average is tops. She was elected the county's outstanding foster grandparent of the year, and the project director's evaluation gave her an Above Average in all categories, including alertness, initiative, appearance, quality of service, relationship with other foster grandparents—and Excellent in overall evaluation.

Her family has not been surprised at these kudos. Born in Boston and the mother of four strapping sons, her half-dozen grandchildren all up north, Helen keeps telling the clan by phone and letter that she'd like to get on top of the tallest building in Tallahassee and "yell out about how great is the Foster Grandparent Program." She talks often and long about opportunity for older people to develop talents that have been suppressed, of her belief that mental power is the most precious and distinguished possession of the elderly and therefore should be developed to its fullest.

The FGP gives Helen the sort of life she likes best, that of service to others. Before she was forcibly retired at sixty-five, she worked in the housekeeping department at St. Luke's Hospital in Jacksonville. After weeks without work, she grew restive and volunteered to serve meals at the YMCA; and when she signed up for the FGP, they put her on the Jacksonville waiting list. Upon moving to Tallahassee, she was accepted immediately, and when her success with little Christy was noted, the program wanted to put her into the public schools, using her as a model for the good the elderly could do there. But the idea was slow to blossom, and Helen worked three years with Sheila before she was transferred in 1980 from the hospital to a local high school to work with emotionally disturbed boys between fourteen and nineteen years of age.

The "firecracker" went to work immediately and found it a tougher job than she had anticipated. The boys were involved in drugs, and instead of working when they came to school, they went to sleep on top of the tables. Most had been rejected and abused, and although they were starving for affection, Helen approached them slowly. Any mother of four sons knows well that teenage boys are embarrassed by a physical show of affection, and Helen hooked them with the gumdrops she carried with her. One gumdrop for one kiss became the rule, and they came to know that they had to pay for the gumdrop. She was soon "grandma" to them all, and they kissed her without shame.

There was nineteen-year-old Luke who had developed a crush on a young teacher, and one day, his face flushed, he confided in Helen about his obsession. They were having lunch in the cafeteria when he suddenly turned to her and said, "Grandma, I've got to rape Mrs. Webster."

Helen stood up from the table. "Come on, Luke, you and I are going to take a walk." Outside, she told him, "You just don't do that. You needn't be ashamed, because your feelings are natural. But Luke, you've got to think up a way to direct this emotion so you don't end up in prison." After twenty minutes she had settled him down. Her report resulted in Luke's removal from Mrs. Webster's class, and he later graduated from high school, is now working at a restaurant job, and has phoned Helen to tell her he has saved enough money to go to California.

There was Johnny. At fourteen the boy was underweight and rundown, and his face was devoid of color. Helen did not let him know she was aware of his history. Three years earlier he had shot and killed his sister and ever since had refused to discuss it with anyone, including lawyers, doctors, and therapists. Helen often joined him for walks, and one day as they sat on a bench in the sun, she took his hand and said, "Johnny, I'm your friend, and I want you to know that any time you want to talk, I'm here to listen. You can trust me."

Johnny broke into sobs and told her about the shooting. From his account it was impossible to tell if it had been deliberate or an accident, but to Helen the important thing was the guilt the boy carried within himself. He seemed to want to be punished; he had begun to steal, to get in all kinds of trouble, and it was the opinion of school counselors that he hoped to be apprehended for these petty crimes.

At home, he had his wish for punishment. His mother

nagged at him day and night about his sister's death. His father put on heavy boots and kicked the boy; he handcuffed him to the family car and then beat him without mercy.

"Do you believe in God?" Helen asked him.

He seemed insulted. "Of course I believe in God!"

"Then look at it this way, Johnny. Your sister is up in heaven, and she can see everything you do. Do you think she is proud of you when she sees you steal? When you get into trouble with the law? Don't you think she'd forgive you a lot sooner if you were a good boy?"

As December approached that year, Helen asked him what he wanted for Christmas.

"To die," said Johnny.

The following Monday he was absent from school, and when Helen returned to her apartment, she immediately called Johnny's home to ask where he was.

"He's in the hospital," said the boy's father.

"Which one?"

He didn't know and turned to ask his wife who then came to the phone. "Johnny tried to commit suicide last night," she said.

At the hospital Helen found the boy unable to speak and breathing with difficulty. His face was a vivid red. He had taken aspirin tablets at midnight, and his parents hadn't gotten him to the hospital until late that morning. Because he had swallowed the pills with the help of beer, doctors had been unable to pump his stomach. While Helen stood at his bedside, a nurse told her that Johnny's mother was coming to see him, and Helen stepped aside to avoid meeting the woman face to face. But she heard her; Johnny's mother screamed at him, berating him for causing her so much trouble.

As Sheila had been "my Sheila" Johnny had become "my Johnny," and Helen convinced the hospital staff that the boy should be evaluated psychiatrically. This was done, and it was found he needed help. But there was no facility available for him at the time. Helen steamed to the rescue once Johnny was well enough to return to school. She contacted the proper authorities, Johnny's parents were taken to court, and he was removed from their home. Two months ago she visited him on his birthday in the pleasant surroundings of a home for disturbed boys. At sixteen, Johnny is cheerful and robust, and he is learning to be a welder in anticipation of the day he will be released. "Another victory for the FGP," crows Helen.

Working at the high school, she didn't expect miracles; she wanted only to see improvement, however small. After what she considered had been good weeks, she gave parties for the boys—parties such as they have never known.

"All you kids are going to be executives," she told them. "Big shots. And executives have to know how to eat fancy kinds of food when it's served, so you don't just sit there and wonder what to do with it."

She cooked at home and took the food to school and laughed delightedly when the boys stared as she lifted the covers. She served snails and told them how to pronounce *escargots*. She taught them how to eat artichokes. She brought squid, even octopus. Some turned up their noses, preferring hot dogs, but many were interested and all but dove into the food.

"This will never do," said Helen. She brought a tablecloth and flowers for a centerpiece and taught them to sit and enjoy each other's company at table, and the kids loved "all the gentleman stuff." The boy with the best overall improvement during a month was then taken out to dinner by Helen at any restaurant he named. She prayed none would name the most expensive restaurant in town. "But if a boy had, I'd have taken him there," she says. "I don't spend money on cigarettes or liquor or snuff, and the few dollars I spend on their dinners is to me a better investment than an IRA. Because it's working for a human being."

Last fall Helen was transferred once more, this time to

work within the school system with boys seven to eleven years old. She's still spending her own money. In the elementary school, she feels so sorry for the children living in squalid homes that she bought a football and put it up front where all could see it. "I've made a chart," she told them, "and on that chart goes a cross for every day you're good and a star for a super day. Whoever has the most stars by the end of the month gets the football. Next month, it'll be a catcher's glove and a baseball."

Helen loves the bribery and so do the kids. In the matter of bribery, she's back with the gumdrop routine, collecting kisses every day.

She's also back with Sheila, still visiting her at the hospital where the girl will live out her days. Helen has never given up on "my Sheila." Back in the years when the girl was her foster grandchild, Helen was irked every time the hospital sent Sheila's mother a necessary form for signature and it was returned without a word of inquiry about the child. After a while Helen couldn't stand what she felt was heartless abandonment of Sheila and asked for permission to write the girl's mother.

But first she did a lot of reading about parents of mentally retarded children, wanting to find out if there could possibly be a good reason for the indifference that so exasperated her. She learned it is sometimes shame, sometimes unbearable sorrow, sometimes real absence of love. Parents are frequently divorced because of a mentally retarded child, each blaming the other for faulty genes. But most often it is a sense of guilt that keeps parents away. Hard as it is to realize, many people believe that God has punished them for their sins by giving them an imperfect child.

"Nonsense!" snorted Helen, and sat down to write Sheila's mother with considerably more understanding than she'd had prior to her research. In her letter she said that Sheila was getting along beautifully, that she was in good hands, and that she was loved. Helen enclosed a recent picture of the child and herself.

"I've been reading up about the parents," she wrote, "and I want to tell you I understand. It's getting better in the world because people are being educated to understand and accept. We know you couldn't take care of Sheila, but I want you to know that I love her very much. You don't have to worry about her because as long as I'm around, I'll take care of her."

To the amazement of the hospital staff, the mother not only replied with a lovely letter to Helen but some months later went to the hospital to see her daughter for the first time since she had left her there. Helen was not present at the meeting; it was better that the reunion be a private one. But she was overjoyed that the mother had seen Sheila. "Now the woman can go to bed without being sick inside her heart, because now she knows that Sheila has loving care."

As has been true all her life, Helen plans on continuing to serve. "I just pray that God gives me my health for another twenty years. Even if I have to use a walker to get there when I'm ninety-three, I'll want to go and be with my kids every day."

CONCHA

Concha de Gonzalez. A long name for a birdlike woman exactly five feet tall, and a name as proud as Concha herself. The longtime widow of a Guatemalan ambassador to the United Nations, Concha is imbued with pride that is not conceit but rather the elation of knowing she is a lady. A lady, as defined in the culture of Concha's girlhood, is a woman known for her consideration of other human beings, and Concha works at that.

Her tiny apartment on a windswept street on San Francisco's west side is filled with photographs of her two sons, their wives and children, and over the mantel is an oil portrait of her late husband in white tie, his chest blazing with diplomatic ribbons. Pictures are not enough to fill a life, however, particularly that of a woman who so loves children that she planned for seven of her own. After her sons were grown, she tried to rectify the situation by adopting a little girl, but because of her age was told she could only have a teenager. Her sons advised against that, and so Concha continued with what she considered an empty life until she was sixty-nine and read in a newspaper about the Foster Grandparent Program.

That was four years ago, and there was disappoint-
ment, because there were no openings at that time for a
grandparent. Concha was put on a waiting list, but not
content to only sit and wait, she attended all of the orientation meetings and in addition enrolled in classes training
people to work with abused children.

So it was that when the Family Service Agency of San
Francisco decided to work in the area of neglected children,
they assigned Concha as a foster grandmother. She was to
work in what was called a respite home, a temporary haven
for kids whose parents were having problems that ad-
versely affected home life.

They came in droves. It has been estimated that in the
past three years, 350 children have passed through the
respite home. In this sort of work, instead of the usual foster grandparent assignment of two children each day (one
in the morning, one in the afternoon), Concha has dealt
with a steady stream of youngsters, some of whom came to
the home for as little as one day.

It's a particularly difficult thing to deal with children
without having the time to learn and understand the
background that has sent them to the home. Concha says,
"All you can do is to try to make them understand there is
someone who cares, who loves them, even for a day."

The goal of the respite home is to keep together families
that are failing and to repair those that have already broken
up. Giving the children a refuge helps them to escape temporarily from an atmosphere of misery, and it is often helpful to
the parents to be free of the children for a period perhaps long
enough to mend their differences, cure their ills.

Every morning and afternoon there are new small
faces. There was Sally, and she comes still, showing up
every once in a while, sent there for reasons the staff has
still to fathom. And every time Sally arrives she has re-
gressed from the former stay. Eight years old, she carries a
baby's milk bottle and stands at the entrance, not moving,
not speaking, just sucking at the milk and staring.

"Would you like me to comb your hair?" Concha asks and then does what she does with them all—makes the child understand that someone cares. After a while Sally seems normal, playing with toys and with the other children. But Concha knows that when Sally returns, there will again be the vacant stare, the deep unhappiness, that the girl will again have forgotten how to play.

There are the twins, Ralph and Ruthie, whose parents have recently been divorced. Ralph adores his father and is too young to accept the vacuum caused by his father's absence. Ralph translates this absence as desertion and therefore feels his father no longer loves him. He reacts with a deep anger toward everyone and everything. "I don't like the food," he says, and his sister apes him. "Me neither." He is told to pick up some toys and he stamps his foot. Ruth stamps hers. She follows her brother's every reaction, making it doubly difficult for Concha to bring the twins to the point where she can evince her love.

She comprehends Ralph's rage; Concha herself was a child of divorce, which in her case resulted in alienation from her mother. Concha's father had dark eyes and hair, and the fact that she resembled him was her misfortune. Concha's mother was a beautiful woman, blonde, blue eyed, fair skinned; and her favorite child was her blond, blue-eyed son who lived with her in the United States. Concha, so reminiscent of the divorced husband, was sent to live with her grandparents in Guatemala. Yes, she understands Ralph's behavior.

Yet Concha doesn't brim with sentiment. The children know her as the dependable little lady who's always there to help and to hug (only if they want a hug—Concha believes in letting the child make the first move), but they also know not to push her too far.

"I don't consider myself a patient woman," she says. "The Spanish comes up in me, and I can be very stubborn. With Tommy, for instance. His mother lost her first child in a crib death and has been so terrified of losing Tommy that she has carried him all his life. At night she would go into his room and wake him to see if he was all right. So Tommy got to the point where he had to be carried and wouldn't do anything for himself. When he came to the respite home, I made up my mind not to touch him. If he wanted something, he'd have to get it for himself. This child weighed perhaps fifty pounds and would stand in front of me wanting to be picked up. I said no, he said yes, I said no. When he wanted to be lifted onto a chair, I told him to get onto it himself. He said no, I said yes. It went on like that for three days before we broke the emotional dependence." Concha smiles. "I think the Spanish helps. Maybe that's why it all works well at the respite home."

She is appalled at the bad manners of many of the children. While not expecting them to know the finer points of courtesy, she is adamant that they at least know how to use utensils at the table. "The way they eat! So many live in campers, roughing it, I suppose you'd call it. They've never used a fork or spoon. Give them noodles and in goes the hand. It's easier for the mother that way, you see—she doesn't have to wash as many dishes." Concha teaches them "what is right" in the hope that some of it will stay with them.

She says that being a foster grandmother has taught her to be less rigid. "At first I was horrified at the terrible things that went on in these families, but now I think I have a better understanding. Not every woman can be a mother, you see. We can have the babies, but whether or not we're able to rear them properly is an entirely different question.

Concha's work has been meaningful, from caring for a child to give the depressed mother time to straighten out her life to Barbara, the respite home's record-breaking visitor, who stayed two whole months while doctors attempted to cure her mother's mental illness.

These small steps are in fact potential victories. We must face the reality that there are American homes where violence is the rule rather than the exception; where parents drink themselves into unconsciousness; where parents fill their bodies with drugs until they are senseless; where, in short, there is no love for the children. America can scarcely expect children caught in such situations to grow into decent and law abiding adults. Without love, it is probable they will in turn withhold affection from their own mates and offspring and very likely the world. And so every child who is saved through the knowledge that there are people who *do* care gives hope for a responsible citizen of the future.

Concha loves them all, remembers them all. Much like the English nanny, she loves and yet one day has that love taken from her. She has trained herself to turn aside from the emotion when yet another child goes out the door for the last time; she tells herself there will be another child tomorrow.

She is a lady of spirit, and it was broken only once that I know of. Seven years ago, returning home from her selling job at a department store, Concha left the bus and was walking toward her apartment when a mugger attacked her from behind, dragging her along the street and breaking both her arm and shoulder. The resultant pain put her out of commission for several weeks and, more important, put a dent in her faith in the ultimate goodness of humanity. After twenty-eight years of working at the store, she decided she was, at sixty-five, too old to cope with a fulltime job in today's world.

Typically, she blamed herself in part. "I had been taking karate lessons for a couple of years. If I'd seen that boy coming at me from behind, I could have taken care of him. I don't have a belt as yet, but I'm told I have a very good back kick."

ANGELA

As far as I know, Angela Ulinski holds the Foster Grandparent Program record as a biological grandmother. At sixty-three, she has thirty-five grandchildren and four great-grandchildren of her own; enough, one would think, so that Angela wouldn't need to go out and look for more.

Following five years of caring for an ill husband, Angela was widowed when she was only forty-two years old and went to work to support her eight children. There was no opportunity for remarriage. "Who wants a woman with eight kids?" she says with a giggle. She had no skills, so she did housework for others and held jobs in factories. Such work seemed perfectly natural to Angela, a first-generation American whose parents had come from Poland before the turn of the century, expecting gold in the streets and finding dust instead.

Angela remembers her childhood with both nostalgia and great pride. "There were fourteen of us to support, and in those days, immigrants would take any job they could get, sometimes for fifty cents an hour." In Toledo, where her parents had married after meeting in their mutual boarding house, her father earned a living by unloading coal at the docks. He pushed the heavy wheelbarrows for up to twelve hours a day, straining, at one point in his route, to shove the heavy load over raised railroad tracks.

"When he came home at night," recalls Angela, "his hands were so swollen that our mother had to pry them open and rub them with warm water."

Her parents studied America's history, the Constitution, and the Bill of Rights and became naturalized citizens. "If one of us mispronounced an English word, mom would smack us," says Angela. The pride in becoming Americans was tremendous and lingers to this day.

"America was built by the immigrants," says Angela Ulinski. "The Irish and the Poles, the Italians and Germans." She wonders aloud at the miracle of Toledo's St. Patrick's cathedral, "those heavy stones raised as if to the heavens by all those derelicts."

Angela was sixty-six years old before she joined the FGP. Her reason for joining, in truth, was not because she wanted more children around her. There were enough of those to help populate Toledo, but with her Social Security benefits beginning in 1974, Angela figured she deserved a breather. But the breather lasted only a year before she found time was most definitely hanging heavy on her hands. When she applied, the FGP accepted her because they needed someone to drive, but then almost immediately they put her to work in the home for severely retarded children.

Angela is a singular foster grandparent in that she is candid about her early misgivings regarding these children—and fiercely protective of them. Defensive would actually be a better description. "I don't discuss these kids with neighbors or friends," Angela says, "because most people just don't understand about them." Yet at the beginning, Angela had self doubts that early on included withdrawal from these children who were flat on their backs "and some so deformed they were hard to look at." There were seven other foster grandparents at the home, and Angela watched them feed the retarded youngsters who more often than not spit the food out, sometimes all over the grandparents.

What was she doing here? Angela asked herself. At first she thought about how she'd spent her life raising a big family and so didn't need this sort of hassle. Then, gradually, her question became, "What can I do for these children?"

She soon found out when she was assigned her two daily youngsters. She learned that if she stroked an arm or the neck of a child, even for a minute, this would give the child pleasure. She learned that although the mentally retarded live in a world all their own, they know quite well when someone is being kind to them. And when someone is being mean to them. The first children assigned to her lived until they were seven years old. One, blind and hydrocephalic, joined Angela in singing; he could say the alphabet forward and backward. When he died, his mother came to talk to the staff after the funeral. "I hope you don't think unkindly of me because I have not come to see him," she told them. "But after he was born, I just couldn't take it, couldn't accept it. I was angry with God, and I couldn't look at him."

Angela feels differently: "He was the sweetest child you could ever want to know. If I came to his bed in the morning and purposely stayed quiet to see what he would do, he'd say, 'Well, say something!' He knew when I was there, even though he was blind. And if I didn't exercise him, he'd demand it. 'Exercise!' he'd say."

But it was Mindy who was, and still is, the triumph of Angela's seven years in the Foster Grandparent Program. Angela progressed from a woman standing on the outside and looking in at these 'different' children to becoming the epitome of her name—an angel who is happy about having learned what she *can* do for these youngsters.

Mindy was six years old when Angela began working with her. The child was confined to a wheelchair, her diagnosis—severe mental retardation; her prognosis—no hope. "You will not be able to effect much change with this child," Angela was told. Mindy was unable to speak or even cry. If unhappy, she could only emit a small meow; Angela learned this is the *cri du chat* (cry of the cat) syndrome. She asked for literature on the subject and learned that the pitiful sound is the only one that can be made by some microcephalic children; it is present at birth and persists until five months of age or longer. With Mindy it had lasted for several years. The first time Angela saw her, the little girl was feeding herself, tossing the food at such a rapid rate that she couldn't manage to eat half of it. Angela went to her and held the child's hand, guiding it slowly to Mindy's mouth.

"Why are you doing that?" an aide asked. "She's supposed to feed herself."

"I know," said Angela, "but I want to slow her down." And she did.

Patience is the key word. "You cannot be impatient with these children," says Angela. "You must face the fact it can take months to teach them just to tie a shoelace. If you do get impatient, you will feel ashamed of yourself."

With her mountain of patience Angela proceeded to teach Mindy to walk. She wheeled her into a big room where she put mats on the floor and then placed the girl prone onto a mat. Angela got down on the mat on her hands and knees and put a toy just out of Mindy's reach.

"Come on, Mindy, get it!"

The child would reach and wriggle, and if and when she managed to get close to the toy, Angela would move it a little farther away. Mindy would whimper a little but after a while try again.

"Come on, Mindy. You can do it!"

It took six months, but Mindy learned to crawl. ("Boring, yes," says Angela, "but the funny thing is that the six months went by before I knew it.")

Soon after, Angela asked staff members to watch, and they were astonished and pleased and put Mindy into the programming classes where she had the attention of trained staff. They asked Angela to attend these classes with Mindy who by that time could raise herself to a kneeling position.

They decided Mindy was now too heavy for Angela to handle, and two months after having assigned her another child, they called Angela back to come and see Mindy. When Angela walked into the room, the child was not only standing, but wobbling from one leg to the other while staff members held her hands. Today Mindy walks with a walker and without a foster grandparent because her improvement is such that she is under the wing of a specially trained teacher.

"When I see her in the halls, walking all alone with her walker," says Angela, "I'll pat her butt and say, 'Come on Mindy, get going!' And you know what? She giggles. She doesn't meow any more, she giggles. It's so rewarding to hear her laugh."

Angela's patience is even further tested when she works with no progress at all. Her work with Violet is an example and symbolic of all the thousands of unsung foster grandparents who serve so steadfastly.

"Vi isn't a syndrome—she was brain damaged at birth although they gave her artificial respiration for almost a half hour," says Angela. "She's fifteen years old now, and the one foot that's turned inward is getting worse. She has a dislocated hip, and they keep a block between her legs to separate the bone and a block across the foot to keep it from turning in. She can't feed herself. There's no hope of her ever standing up. Because of her brain damage, she can't cooperate in any way.

"There was a time when I would wonder what in the

world I could do for this child. But now I know how much she loves the feel of fresh air and sunshine, and I take her for strolls outdoors in her wheelchair. Like the other kids, she responds to petting baby animals in the zoo, and I take her there. I give her back rubs. I clap her hands to the rhythm of music. She can't understand what I read to her, but I read aloud anyway because I know she enjoys the sound of my voice. The only progress in the six years I've been with Vi is the fact she recognizes me and is happy when I come to talk with her. I'm sure that she loves me.

"I wish I could explain all this to the world, but I can't. My family brags about what I do here, but even they, most of them, won't come and look at the children. People don't understand, you see. Unless you've worked with these children, I guess it's just impossible to understand."

Nonetheless, it is true that family and neighbors admire Angela for her work as a foster grandparent. And in Toledo, her friends think she is something special for being the mother of eight and the grandmother of thirty-five children. "Eight kids!" they say. "You've done your job for God and country."

Angela shakes her head. "God did it for *me*. But yes, I had all those kids for my country. I'm proud of them for contributing to America, and I'm proud of the grandchildren who all are making a fine place for themselves in this great country."

ALLEAN

For the abused and neglected children in Missouri's rural Polk County, Allean Barnhouse is, in many cases, the one sane person in their lives, an oasis of calm and caring in an unhappy existence. Allean became a nurse's aide after her husband died eighteen years ago and until she became a foster grandparent, worked with elderly as well as caring for the babies in a church nursery. The experience gave Allean a lot of the moxie that supports her today in her work for the Foster Grandparent Program.

Polk County embraces poor and rocky soil; it is one of the lesser blessed districts of the Ozarks, and its people seem to have more problems than most. Allean is sent into their homes—with their permission, of course—to offer help where help is needed.

Despite the human misery she tries to assuage, Allean finds that one of her most difficult hurdles is the need to stay unruffled when faced with homes that are unkempt and often filthy. "They are not all that way, mind you—some of the houses shine all over, but many's the time I've stood by a bed and hoped nothing would come out from underneath it to bite me."

In former years, when she was nursing the elderly or babies, Allean was what she describes as a finicky woman; she had raised her eight children in a spotless home. It has therefore required a lot of self-control when facing kitchens spilling over with soiled dishes and spoiled food, unmade beds heaped with everything imaginable. At the beginning of her assignment with the FGP, she often had to turn her face away so that residents would not realize she was gagging. With time she has learned to conquer the nausea and, with rare tact, ignore the grime and pretend instead that she is in a castle.

The ability makes her special. She is accepted by parents in their homes because she never shows disapproval, never looks down her nose, or puts on airs. She confines the purpose of her visits to the urgent need for help.

There is a woman in Polk County, for example, who is without a husband and trying to care for a preteenage son who is slightly retarded. The mother is obese, and ever since Allean discovered the woman and the boy are sleeping in one bed—the only bed in the house and a narrow one at that—she has been canvassing the area for a donation of a second bed.

"I hope," she says, "this sort of thing isn't taking responsibility away from the parents, but I get so *involved!*"

She also has the tact to avoid the jealousy or the wrath of the parents. She teaches children about personal cleanliness, but even here she must toe the line; if youngsters begin making a point of scrubbing the house and bathing, things seldom practiced by their elders, it is often the case that the parents grow angry at her interference.

Allean's talent for going about her job quietly is responsible for her total acceptance by the parents. One father has told authorities that Allean is the only woman he will allow in his house. "Don't send anybody else!" he warns.

She goes into homes where a mother has walked out

on a brood of children and disappeared, and Allean helps the distraught father to care for the kids. There are many homes where the father has left and a mother is struggling to raise the children alone. One of these, Allean happily reports, "keeps a half-dozen children looking as though they had just stepped out of a bandbox."

But tidiness is the exception to the rule. Although she is invited to stay for dinner in most of the homes, Allean declines with a polite excuse. In one home she was bitten by an unidentified creature and developed a persistent case of impetigo, which she steadfastly failed to report to authorities.

There is seldom an idle moment during her visits. One day when she had taken children to the park for ice cream, their mother joined them and suddenly said, "I think I'm going to go out." Allean realized the woman was having an epileptic seizure and took the proper steps, following up with arrangements for medication.

Some families just dissolve in misery. One father left home for another woman, and his departure severely affected one of his daughters. Allean did all she could to comfort the mother, but the woman went berserk soon after and subsequently disappeared, leaving her six children in charge of the eldest. On her next visit, Allean found the little ones dependent on a ten-year-old boy.

She drives children to doctor and dentist appointments, she brushes their hair, reads to them, plays games with them, gives them a thorough bath when she can get away with it. In good weather she takes them to a park to play and sometimes to her own home overnight—an excellent ploy to effect a bath. She almost always gives them a little treat, a small gift. "Sure, out of my pocket, but never enough to hurt."

Allean finds the subject of abused children very difficult. She doesn't know about other places, but where she works it is often the case that children are afraid to report the brutality of their parents. "They train the kids very carefully," she says. "The children are afraid to talk, fearing retaliation. And lots of them really don't *want* to be taken away from their parents. They accept whatever their life is like. It's all they've ever known."

She has read everything she's been able to find on the subject of abused children and, as a nurse, knows what to look for in the way of telltale signs on a child's body.

Many children in Polk County may be deprived of material things, but they are blessed in having the sharp eye, the loving hands, and the extraordinary tact of foster grandmother Allean Barnhouse.

BERTHA

Try to imagine a nine-year-old boy weighing only fifteen pounds. Brian would have been normal except for the tragedy of brain damage at birth, and were it not for that, perhaps his mother wouldn't have deserted her family. When Brian was five, with an older sister and brother and a younger brother, his mother simply walked out from under the weight of her responsibilities. Four young children are handful enough without the care of one child who is physically deformed and mentally deficient.

Afterward, the father took the boy to two different hospitals where little was done for him before Brian's lucky admittance to the Belle Chasse State School in Louisiana.

Enter Bertha Hoyt, brand-new foster grandmother.

Bertha was sixty-five years old when she joined the FGP in 1972 and matriarch of thirty progeny, including her great-grandchildren. When asked what kind of children she wanted to work with at the school, she answered that she wanted to help those who couldn't help themselves. She proved her sincerity the morning the director of nursing told four new foster grandparents the story of Brian and the desertion of his mother, then asked if any of them would take him.

"I will," said Bertha.

She remembers that she was close to tears "looking at that little bundle of nothing lying in that old homemade wheelchair," and she was overcome by a compulsion to do something for the child.

She's been with Brian ever since, and in the intervening ten years the boy's progress has astonished the doctors. When Brian was first admitted they felt he was fairly hopeless because of the serious degree of his brain damage and could only hope that with help he might be able to reach a higher level of awareness. Almost immediately the boy was quite aware of Bertha, to the point that he cried when she left the room.

He had refused to eat for the nurses, but Bertha had the time for patience, and time is a luxury few nurses ever have. It required an extraordinarily long time to feed Brian whose habit of "tongue thrusting" made it difficult to put food into his mouth. Bertha figured the spoon could go in sideways, and it did. Further, Brian seemed to want to please her.

In one year his weight had tripled.

No one at the hospital even dreamed he would make such progress. But typical in their dedication, the staff felt that Brian, like every individual, had a basic right to be helped so that he could reach his maximum potential. This has proved to be a condition in which he is alert, recognizes his surroundings, and interacts with nurses and therapists as well as his foster grandmother. He still has difficulty in reaching for objects because of his deformity, but he has reached a point of intelligence where he will soon begin a program in which he will be taught to respond to a yes or no situation by signaling with his head or his eyes.

Ten years after Bertha's start with him, Brian weighs

sixty-five pounds. His face is beautiful—deep blue eyes, a creamy complexion, and a crop of thick, dark hair, which has recently been cut and styled by a local barber. Brian laughed with glee when his hair was blown dry. You might think of his sixty-five pounds as so little for a young man now nineteen years old, but it should be remembered that his weight has quadrupled. Bertha has been there ounce by ounce, writing a monthly report regarding his weight, so dedicated that she buttonholes staff to announce proudly, "Brian gained two ounces this week!" The staff teases her that they try to dodge her in the halls, knowing their work will be held up while she rhapsodizes about Brian.

It is acknowledged that Bertha herself is the basic reason Brian has made such spectacular headway. She has been away from him only once in the ten-year period, and that was a spell of five months when she was ill and could not go to the school at all. During that time Brian was assigned to another foster grandmother, but the magic just wasn't there, and he again began refusing to eat and lost weight. When Bertha regained her strength, she phoned to say she wanted to return if there was an opening. They called her back in the following Monday morning and asked her to feed Brian both his breakfast and dinner for three weeks. He beamed happily at the sight of her and ate one of the biggest meals of his life.

Brian's siblings, all normal, and his father visit Brian regularly at the school. The father has never remarried and seems devoted to the boy, wishing he could occasionally have Brian at home. But care of the boy is beyond the family's ability, and so they are cheered by the frequency with which Brian is taken for weekends to homes of nurses and therapists, several of whom lined up for the privilege once Brian was pronounced well enough to be taken from the school for short periods. Said one therapist, "He's such a happy kid, it's a joy to have him in the house."

Once, very quietly, Brian's mother appeared at the

school and asked to see him. She had heard of the miraculous change and wanted to see for herself if the rumors were true.

The Foster Grandparent Program began at Belle Chasse in 1972, and Bertha was the first to fill out an application. For a few years after her husband's death in an accident, Bertha continued the family poultry and egg business. But once she had sold it, she was restless for something to do, and the answer came to her from, of all places, her church. One of her grandsons, who served as an altar boy at the church, had found an application for potential foster grandparents.

"You see who sent me here," smiles Bertha Hoyt.

OGLE

There are two things about Ogle Boyer's life that make him a standout. The first is that he has spent sixty of his seventy-nine years in jail. The second is that he is the first parolee to serve as a foster grandparent.

Ogle has no excuse, no reason for his life of crime, which began when he was eighteen years old and was arrested for petty theft. He was sentenced to thirty days, and three months after he was released from prison, he stole some watches, hoping to sell them for food and went back into the Indiana State Penitentiary for several years. In those days there were no halfway houses, no juvenile halls, no correctional facilities for the young. The slightest offense often sent a youngster into a prison alongside hardened criminals. And Ogle learned from the older prisoners.

It was the beginning of his personal crime wave, and this made him different way back in 1922, because Ogle had two brothers who always steered clear of trouble, even though they shared equally in the misery of the Boyer family's existence.

"We had a rotten daddy," says Ogle. "He stayed drunk all the time and wouldn't take care of his family. My brothers went straight, and I went wrong. I don't know why it happened, but I've always believed my daddy's meanness just came out in me. Like a cancer."

With only four years of schooling "in a corn field in the Indiana hills," Ogle set his course for prison. He was convicted for grand larceny, breaking and entering, armed robbery, assault and battery, and attempted rape. (In the twenties if a burglar broke into a house after dark, it was "assumed" his intent was rape, and that was frequently the recorded offense.)

His sentences varied—ten, three, twenty years. Ogle existed in one prison after another—Michigan City, Jeffersonville, Pendleton, Franklin, and some that no longer exist. In his younger years he was occasionally released by a parole board prior to serving a full sentence, but Ogle always went right back in.

"You went back in," he says, "because there wasn't no other place to go. You had a record so you couldn't get a job. God made you so you need to eat and you need to sleep, and you got to have money for those things. So you broke a couple of windows 'cause you knew that'd get you a bed and a couple of meals maybe. Prison ain't no grand place let me tell you, but if you got no place else to go, it's better than nothing."

His last sentence, the big one, was for thirty years, after he committed what was then called in Ohio "night season." If a man broke into an inhabited house between six o'clock in the evening and six o'clock in the morning, the law assumed he intended bodily harm to the residents, and so in March of 1952 Ogle went into prison and stayed there. He became a seasoned criminal, an expert in avoiding punishment by the guards and injury by other inmates.

One would suppose that a man with Ogle Boyer's

criminal record and years of imprisonment might look like a frightening creature, hulking and hideous. The surprise of Ogle is that he resembles America's most beloved character, Santa Claus. Snow-white hair flows over his collar, his complexion is a healthy pink, smooth cheeks are free of wrinkles, and his eyes *are* the eyes of Santa, a clear blue with an almost constant twinkle that well matches his frequent chuckle. I describe the twinkle as 'almost constant' because at times Ogle Boyer's eyes fill with tears, tears of compassion, unexpected from an apparent villain.

There was a point during his incarceration, says Ogle, during which his basic attitudes were totally reversed. "Two years, five years in prison didn't do it," he says. "I'd get out on parole and go right back. I held the record for seeing the parole board—thirteen times. I'd get five years, ninety days, another five, kept goin' back and forth, and those short sentences never cured me.

"Then, after about twenty-five years, all of a sudden I wanted to do right. I wanted to get out and show people, do something for the public. The long years took the ornerisness out of me, took the crime out. But in the long run it took *everything* out of me. After thirty years I just plain didn't care. I told myself if they don't call me up to the parole board any more, I'll just give up and stay here 'til I die."

The parole board hadn't called him up for so many years that the only freedom Ogle had known was in 1972 when he was transferred by a security vehicle from the Ohio State Penitentiary to the prison at Chillicothe, Ohio. He was seventy-seven years old when he was called up once again, and he walked into the office with his shoulders slumped in utter resignation. He had surrendered; it would be far easier just to give up and stay in jail.

"How you feeling?" asked the parole officer.

"Okay."

"I'm giving you parole."

Ogle was stunned. His knees began to shake inside the shapeless prison trousers. He managed to make conversation and appear intelligent until he got out into the hall, and then he stood stock still, feeling the sweat run down his back. They were going to let him out. Now, when he was pushing eighty. He had never known such fright, not even in the prison riots. The emotion seemed to wring out everything inside him, and he almost toppled when the old dizziness swept over him—the loss of balance he suffered from having lived so many years in cages.

They had released him because, finally, there was a halfway house up in Columbus that offered released convicts a place to stay until they could be responsible for themselves. Ogle was given the money he had saved from thirty years of prison jobs—$1,024.70—and a slip of paper with the address of Alvis House on it. An officer drove him from the prison on the outskirts of Chillicothe to the town itself and left him at the bus stop.

He stood on the corner, terrified, and waited more than an hour for a bus to come along. The streamlined automobiles looked so strange, not at all like the boxier cars of the forties. And they went so fast, so many of them. He felt lost and sick to his stomach, and he began to cry. If he could just find a taxi, he'd have the driver take him back to prison, but it seemed as though Chillicothe didn't have any taxis.

Ogle was no longer the strong and confident man who had so often taken the law into his own hands; he was a broken and pitiable old duffer, lonely, confused, and frightened.

When a bus finally came along and pulled up at the intersection, its sign said "Detroit." The door swung open, and the driver said, "Come on, get on!"

Ogle shook his head. "I don't want to go to Detroit. I need to get to Columbus."

"I'm stopping there. Get on!"

Ogle had never seen a bus like it. It was long and wide and gleaming clean, and the seats were unlike anything he'd known in buses so many years ago; there was even a way you could make the seats lean back a little.

He got off in Columbus. It was the first time he'd ever been in the city, and he wondered what to do until a taxi driver asked him where he wanted to go.

"I don't know where it is," said Ogle. He fished the piece of paper out of his pocket. "This says Alvis House."

"Oh, you're one of *them*," said the driver. "I'll take you there."

The ride cost Ogle four dollars and fifty cents, and he wondered if he was being taken advantage of. Back in the forties that much money would buy you a hotel room and a good dinner.

At Alvis House they had no room for Ogle. "You'll have to go to the YMCA," they said.

"Where's that?"

They called a taxi, and that was another four dollars and fifty cents. Ogle figured at that rate he'd be broke in a month. The cab dropped him off at a building, and Ogle went in and stood in the hall, waiting for an elevator to take him up to the sixth floor. He waited and waited, wondering what kind of lazy elevator operators they were hiring these days. When the doors finally opened, there was no one inside the elevator, and Ogle started back in fright. A stranger standing nearby noticed the old man and asked him what was the matter.

"I need to get to the sixth floor."

"Well then, get on in and push the button."

"Button?"

It took Ogle a long time to learn about the new world. In truth, he hasn't learned yet. In the streets he sees people smoking marijuana and drinking wine. It's hard to tell men from women, the way people dress. Babies now are fed by bottle instead of the breast. Ogle doesn't think the world has improved much.

There were "big, high buildings like I never saw. And freeways. The speed of everything scares me. Signs in cities tell you when to cross the street and when not. I'm scared all the time. Like trying to buy a pair of pants. In the old days they had clerks to help you, and you didn't dare touch anything, or you might get busted.

"So I went in this store with nice rugs on the floor and stood around waiting until a woman clerk asked what I wanted. I said pants, and she said well go find a pair you like. So I thought I ought to clear the record, and I said, 'Miss, I want to tell you I'm from the penitentiary—thirty years—I don't know nothin' any more, and I gotta have some help here.'"

In Ogle's apartment there is a gas stove. He had to ask the landlady how to turn it on. Everything was new to him; he had to learn about defrosting the "ice box." The bed was so wide, three whole feet across. He hadn't known anything wider than a cot for so long that even the size of the bed frightened him. He felt he didn't belong. Anywhere. It was difficult to talk with people who spoke in a different way from convicts, and they certainly talked about different subjects. He felt abnormal, and still does, in a world so unfamiliar.

Ogle Boyer is far from stupid; in prison he shored up his four years of public school by reading everything he could get his hands on. He describes himself now as pretty well educated about the inside world but not too bright about the outside. "I'm just trying to know how to be respectable," he says.

He looks and acts respectable, and it was in Columbus, to whose citizens he will always be grateful, that he got his start in living his own life for the first time. At the YMCA they gave him a room and bus tickets to get around town to look for work. But before he had a chance to catch his breath, Ogle found himself in front of television cameras. The story of his uninterrupted thirty years in prison and the thirty years preceding them had spread around town, and the local news people phoned the Y to ask if they'd bring Ogle to the studio.

"People were running around all over the place to look at me, poking me to see if I was real. To them it was like I'd come down out of the sky, in the cages all those years. They felt my hair and held my hands and hugged and kissed me, and I was shy, you know, and scared because I couldn't hardly talk to outside people yet. I was really shook up, but when they sat me in front of a microphone, I talked for thirty minutes about prison life, what goes on there and what it does to you."

That's exactly what Ogle has done as a foster grandparent—he tells youngsters who have already committed misdemeanors or crimes what they're headed for if they don't straighten out.

It took a while for Ogle to get into the program. Ohio doesn't allow felons to work for the state, hold public office, or have anything to do with government affairs. The Foster Grandparent Program is a federal program, and so the social workers in Columbus bent their backs to the task of getting special permission for Ogle to be a foster grandfather. Police and FBI records were checked; calls and interviews were made, pleading the fact of his advanced age; and finally Ogle was cleared. After all, he wouldn't be a staff member or on salary; he would be a volunteer receiving only a stipend for his services. Besides, there was the plus factor of Ogle's avowed dedication to helping boys stay out of prison.

The investigation took three months, and in the interim Ogle became acquainted with Columbus. This is a story in itself, and one I'm happy to share with you because it illustrates so well my faith in the innate goodness of the American people. As I wrote in the foreword of this book, Americans have only to hear of a tragedy, of someone needing help, and they open their hearts and their wallets. Ogle learned this in Columbus where he had become recognizable because of his recent television appearance.

"They'd see me on the street and honk the horn and give me money. Black and white, made no difference. They said 'Here, boy, this is the best I can do. God bless you.' They gave me almost five hundred dollars that way."

People would call him at the YMCA, and when they found he was in his room, they would come to see him and give him things. Bus passes, for instance. "Here, Boyer, you can ride now. You won't have to walk."

Ogle's eyes brim a bit, remembering. "That got me to feel better," he says. "I love Columbus 'cause they put me on my feet."

He chafed during the months of waiting to join the FGP. He'd already been told he might be working in some capacity with kids in correctional institutions, and he'd immediately swelled with pride of purpose. "I can do it!" he crowed. "I know what I'm talking about. I'll bet they had the same hardships I had on the outside, and I know crime and criminals, and I'll tell those kids! They'll stay out of prison if they listen to *me*, you wait and see!"

He was so anxious to go to work that he reported for the job the day after he filled out the application for the Foster Grandparent Program. When the authorities finally got him on board, Ogle threw all his energies into his assigned project of putting youths on what he refers to as the right road.

He was astonished and even faintly amused by the innocence of some of the boys, aged fifteen to eighteen, who had absolutely no idea of what jail was like.

"Do you get to go home at night?" one asked.

Ogle roared with laughter. "Go home! Son, you won't see anything that even looks like home for long years to come!"

Some asked him what the guards were like, and Ogle said, "Every guard has three to four hundred cons to watch. There are desperate characters in prison, guys doing three and four life sentences. The guards can't watch everything, but they're concerned about what goes on. They do their best, and if you walk a straight line, you're all right. If you don't, you're gonna get your head busted. You're in there for a crime, son, and if you don't behave, they'll take it out of you."

Ogle decided he would tell them everything there was to tell about life in prison—that he wouldn't hold back anything. He wouldn't elaborate, maybe not even mention, the fact that newer and more humane prisons had been built since those that had held him in his youth. Might as well let them hear the horrors, that sort of telling ought to get to them.

Listen to the telling . . .

"It's a sorrowful place. You're comin' up eighteen so you'd better listen 'cause that's where you're goin'. It's filthy. You're all crowded up. You're so crowded you're gonna get mistreated by the convicts. They're the ones to watch, not the guards. You're not separated. You can steal a bicycle and be in the same cage with a guy who's killed four, five people. They are desperate guys, and they don't like being crowded. They'll stab you, rape you, bash your head in.

"You all get treated alike, no matter what you're in for. In the Ohio State Penitentiary you wash your clothes in the toilet. Always did. You get one bath a week."

(Ogle declines to mention that recent prison reforms have improved the bathing rules; he's not about to pass up a horror story that will deter the boys.)

"It's a different world. There ain't nobody there to help you. You're gonna do that time, and you're gonna have to abide by the rule of the prison and specially of the convicts. You do what they say. There's dope in there, marijuana, cocaine. They carry it in, somehow get it past security. Detectors don't detect dope, just guns; so they smuggle it in, they put it in their pockets, sprinkle it in their hair, put it in places I ain't gonna tell you about. They even somehow get guns in.

"TV? Sure they got them now. Black and white and about eight inches across, and you can look at it when the man tells you you can look. After work. And you'll work;

you don't sit on your bum. Money? They pay you twenty-four bucks a month for the work, and they put back eight bucks of that for your goin' home money. If you die in there—and you probably will—they get to keep your goin' home money.

"I fall over once in a while now. That's because I lost my balance in prison. You live day and night in a space eight feet long and eight feet high and eight feet wide, filled up with four beds and a toilet and a water basin, and you just sit a lot. There ain't nowhere to stretch, and pretty soon you notice yourself all light-headed, and you gotta catch yourself to keep from falling. My apartment now, all that space makes me dizzy; the walls are too far away to steady myself.

"Another thing. I can't taste food no more, not even an onion. The food in prison is rotten. I can't taste, and I can't smell no more, so I just eat because I know I have to. It started twenty years ago, and when I asked a doctor, he said it'd come back some day, but it never has. I'd give a lot to know what a hamburger tastes like.

"Touch is the only sense I got left. I don't hear too good, and I don't see too good, and I'll tell you about that in a minute. But prison does something to a man's senses. Some go crazy, lots kill themselves. Now, about goin' blind. That comes from no real light for so long, in particular when you're in solitary. That's what they call the hole, and it's like a dungeon. It's so dark in there, you gotta watch your eyes when you come out; the light of day is like an explosion.

"I'll tell you about the hole. I ought to know. I been in there like seventy times, once for ten whole days and nights. It's a nightmare. They strip down the cell, nothin' in it. The man gives you a cup of water if he feels like it that day. There ain't no toilet, so you get that picture, right? Like I said, the hole is a nightmare.

"After a while, a man and woman look the same to you. Everybody looks the same. It sometimes takes twenty years to do that to you, but it will happen. And I don't have to tell you what that means. You're gonna get raped, so you might as well make up your mind to it.

"They like to scare you. And a good way is to put you on death row, even though that ain't your sentence, it didn't come from the judge. I know what I'm talking about. I was in death row once for ninety days. They just let you think you're goin' to the chair, and that does something to you. You'll crack up if you're not careful. The cage is real small. You don't get to see nobody. Everything is quiet. Except when the guys talk to you in real low voices. They say, 'I'm waitin'. How many days now?' The way you get food—they bring it and slide it under the door. You get a bath once a week, only in death row they only give you three minutes to shower. The guard stands there with a watch in his hand.

"They got another dandy little punishment. They tear a blanket into twelve-inch strips and put it on the floor of a big, long hall. Then they bring you out of your cage and tell you to stand on that strip of blanket and stare at the wall. For twelve hours. Standin' at attention. And if you put a part of your foot off that blanket, the guard would come out and whop you.

"I been in two different prison riots, and I'm lucky to be living today. In fifty-two in the Ohio pen they had the place on fire, and all the guards got out, and the police came in, and there was shooting and killing and fire and dragging bodies out. In sixty-eight they had another riot, haulin' them outta there in jeeps to the undertakers. They had cops and national guard and everybody. And there was shooting and raping until it got straightened out when they blew the wall down and the roof off C and D block so they could get to the convicts and control them from killin' each other. Everything was on fire; I don't know how I got through it. I been chained up, been in the hole, had no food, I've had it.

"It don't go away, boys. I see it; I dream about it day

and night. Just this mornin', I'm back in a cage and I can see Foster, a black kid who was a pretty nice boy, and I see him in the hole. 'Foster,' I say, 'what you doin' in that hole, all dirty?' And then I wake up sweating, and the bars are still in front of my eyes, so I have to get up and make myself some coffee. You never get it out of you, never. It's always in your head. Sometimes I still think I'm gonna crack up.

"So don't try to run away from here, boys. You stay like they say, and when you go, you go out of here on the right road. You run away and you know what you'll do—no bed, no food, you're gonna knock somebody over for money to stay alive. And they'll send you back. I don't care what you're here for, just behave. And don't run away, boys. Please."

Sometimes Ogle gets so carried away looking at the young faces that stare at him, jaws gaping in both horror and fascination, that his voice breaks and he has to dig for a handkerchief to dab at his eyes. Sometimes—not often but sometimes—he sees some of the boys surreptitiously pressing the heel of a hand to their eyes, and that pleases Ogle, because he knows he's got to them.

The Foster Grandparent Program has become Ogle's whole life; he devotes most of his waking hours to the program. There is enormous demand for him from the youths at the training center so that now, instead of one-to-one relationships, he is rotated in what they call group education. He takes boys, those who can be trusted not to run away, out of the center. He takes them to help work with mentally retarded children and with the elderly in nursing homes. Schoolteachers request that drug addicts be brought to classes to tell students of the danger of drugs, and Ogle's the one who shepherds them. He also takes the boys for walks in the woods and parks, to the zoo, restaurants, the fair, and to church services. He has taken them to sessions of the state legislature, where they talk with representatives and senators.

Ogle is all over the place at the center and at all hours. He can be found in the barbershop (where he has encouraged boys to learn the trade), the cottages where the boys live, the school, the offices of the center, always offering a helping hand. He takes cookies from the kitchen to boys he feels deserve a treat. When youths are to attend church suppers or a service, it is Ogle who gets them "outside clothes" so that they'll look respectable in church. He's been known to deliver outside clothes to youngsters at midnight on Saturdays.

He is given free run of the center despite the fact that Ogle Boyer is still legally on parole. He laughs at the thought. "When I need to take a kid somewhere special on the same day I'm supposed to report, I just call up my parole officer and tell him I can't make it until tomorrow. He don't care much—he's told me be didn't think I could make it on the outside after all those years in the cage, and so he thinks I'm doing pretty well." He chuckles about that and then turns philosophic and adds, "It don't bother me, bein' on parole still. What's the difference? All life is a parole."

Ogle doesn't get, or even think of asking for, more money than his two-dollar hourly stipend for four hours a day. "The money don't worry me. I'm here to help," he says.

He has been on the receiving end of help from other foster grandparents at the training center. They know his story, and he is candid about his shortcomings. When they eat together at the lunch provided free for them, Ogle asks questions. How to eat something, what utensil to use, and, for the times when he gets back to his own apartment, what to buy and how to cook it. Most important, Ogle's contact with contemporaries who are not criminals is teaching him social behavior, which he in turn tries hard to teach to the boys. He is the pet of the other foster grandparents, who share their love with him in the same way they do with the children.

Before Ogle began his shepherding jobs, he did have specific boys assigned to him. There have been perhaps a dozen in all as their stay is usually brief—no more than six months on average.

There was Hudson, an alcoholic and a drug addict. Ogle didn't know what Hudson was "in" for; he has never asked any of the youngsters, because he doesn't care. From his own experience, one is like another. He worked with Hudson for fourteen months, and when Hudson left he got a job in a barber shop. He often calls Ogle now to talk with him. "I think I made a little gentleman out of that one," Ogle beams.

There is Schultz, who also has learned the barber trade. He's still there, telling Ogle that when he gets out he's not going to monkey around with prison. "I'm gonna hit that right road you keep talking about," he vows. And Ogle says, "I believe Schultz. I think he will."

There is Logan, a seventeen-year-old who has been in for murder for almost two years now. His one passion is basketball, and he and Ogle would talk about the NBA statistics. One day Logan said, "Grandpa, I been listening to you. When I get out I'm gonna go straight, and that's a promise." Logan has a while to go before his release from the training center, but in the interim Ogle trusts him and has had him on trips outside. He takes Logan to the home for the mentally retarded, and there the tall young man helps to feed the youngsters ("They're like babies, ain't they, grandpa?") and helps dress them and takes them to the pool for therapy.

"Logan, he's gonna be fine," says Ogle. "I just know it."

There are failures, of course. "There's people natural born; you can't tell 'em nothin'," says Ogle. "Their mama and daddy couldn't learn 'em anything, and so some of them I can't either. They think they know it all. They ain't crazy, but sometimes you think so. But if he's any kind of a kid at all, I can turn him away from the wrong road. Even the kid whose father kept getting him drunk, getting him high on grass, and made him commit a robbery the kid couldn't even remember. The boy whose mama taught him how to burglarize. The alcoholics that are only fifteen years old. The fourteen-year-old kid in there for rape." Here Ogle slaps his knees. "Fourteen! When he told me I like to fell out!"

Social workers strongly discourage foster grandparents from continuing relationships with youngsters incarcerated for crime. Ogle goes his own way on this, knowing full well there are many he'd rather not meet in a dark alley. "If you trust the wrong one and share a room with him at night, you might not wake up in the morning."

He uses the sense bred into him in prison to tell him which boys he can trust. These are the boys he often sees in downtown Columbus. "They holler at me, and some I got to give money, something to eat on. Some have cleaned up real nice; lots lookin' for jobs. They ain't very old; it's hard for them to get a job. Lots don't have a home to go to. The ones that do, lots of times when they're ready to get out of the center and go home, I meet their folks out front. I tell them 'You better take good care of that kid. He can be a good boy, and if you don't watch him he'll go to prison.' They say thank you and that they're glad I showed him the right road. That's all I can do, you see. But I do believe I've educated seventy-five out of every hundred. Educated, that is. The ones that have actually gone straight and I think will stay that way, maybe one out of two."

One day not long ago, at one of the many staff meetings Ogle slips into, an authority was speaking of the good things effected by the Foster Grandparent Program.

"If a grandparent can save only one child," he said, "that grandparent will have done a great thing."

Ogle felt his insides tighten with pride, and he clapped his hands softly in glee. "I can beat that!" he told himself.

KATRINA

W hen they brought him in she noticed him right
away. This one was young like the others, maybe
fifteen, but different because he was so obviously frightened. He had reason to be scared, thought Katrina. He was
so young to have killed a man.

Everybody already knew about the murder. News
travels fast in any small town, but in Maine it spreads like
a fire storm. The day before in a village not very far away, a
store employee had been shot by the owner's son, and that
morning at the detention center word went around that
they were bringing the boy there and that he'd go into the
lockup straight off.

The boy turned out to be six feet fall, a blond youngster whose handsome face was flushed with both fright and
remorse. Katrina saw the latter quite clearly, and she said
to herself, "I'm going to do something to help that boy."

Katrina Jones had been a foster grandmother at the detention center for a couple of years, following her work for
the Foster Grandparent Program at a school for the deaf.
These services were a natural outlet for her in her old age,
because she had had training first as a nurse's aide and

then as a practical nurse, and by now it was second nature for Katrina to take care of people. Her interest in nursing had begun during the year she spent in a sanitarium as a victim of tuberculosis. And then after her husband died, she threw her heart and soul into what was, to her, the reward of nursing.

Quite naturally, the detention center had placed her in the building's infirmary. Here she came to know almost every young offender incarcerated there, since most of them at some time or other had some small need for medical attention. Occasionally, a boy was even allowed to come out of the lockup, one of the thirteen cells reserved for the most serious offenders. Those who behaved themselves were permitted to play games with Katrina, and she broke a rule of her religious belief when she learned how to play a card game called Spades. Cards, Katrina thought, were a very good way to teach kids about numbers, and many of these inmates were shockingly lacking in arithmetic skills. She read to them and with them and told herself, if I can reach just one boy, just one boy, maybe I can save his whole life.

It was fated to be Steve, the young murderer, whom she would save. In the lockup he developed a skin rash resulting from too little light and exercise in his cell. He had been constrained in the six-by-nine foot space for more than three months when doctors ordered him released to the infirmary. This was Katrina's chance. She explained the Foster Grandparent Program to him and told him she had grown up in a town near his own. She repeated to him what she told all the other kids: "I love you, but I don't love your crime."

He told her how ashamed he was of himself, that he didn't understand how he could go on living when he had killed another human being. Katrina spoke to him of religious faith; she brought him a Bible, and he joined her in the sinner's prayer.

Within a period of weeks Steve spilled out his story to

her. His mother had deserted the family before he and his sister had been old enough to start school. His father had brought them up but without close attention, because his time and energy went into earning a living from the stores he owned. In one of them worked a man we'll call Gus who was an alcoholic and frequently stole money from the cash register to finance his drinking. The first time Steve saw this happen and Gus was aware he'd been observed, he beat the boy. "You'll get more than that if you ever open your mouth about this," he told Steve.

Several times Steve was on the scene when Gus dipped into the till. It was hard *not* to observe the theft, as Steve worked alone with Gus at the store every day after school.

"He beat me so badly," Steve told Katrina, "that I was really scared of him. So one night I went home to dinner, and then I came back with a gun."

"A gun! Whatever made you carry a gun?"

"I was afraid he'd beat me again that night, and I wanted the gun to scare him off. So he did—he came for me, and I fired." Steve rubbed both fists into his eyes. "I didn't mean it, Grammy, honest I didn't mean it. I didn't even know he was dead. I thought I'd only hurt him, and I dropped the gun and ran for the police station."

This one *was* different, thought Katrina. He'd had the usual background shared by most of these lads—a one-parent home and that parent too busy to give children attention and affection—but Steve hadn't surrendered his principles. This was the first time he'd ever been arrested, and Katrina was sure he wasn't a bad boy. He'd made one mistake, the very worst one, but it had not been premeditated, and it had been provoked.

In the first three months of Steve's detention he left his cell only to be taken to court. Already lonely and frightened, his emotions were compounded on "court days." Katrina was always there as he left. "Don't worry," she told him. "Everything will turn out all right."

Each time Steve came back to his cell, Katrina was the

first person he wanted to talk to. Again, she would be there. He says now, "It was like having my mother with me. She was wonderful. I needed to talk and she knew it, and she'd show up no matter where I was. Every time I was transferred to a new unit at the center, she'd put in for her own transfer to that unit. They were the toughest years of my life, and she was there every day to pull me through."

By this time Katrina was deeply convinced of the goodness within the boy, and the staff apparently felt the same way, because Steve was given "A" status, which meant they trusted him. He was allowed to attend high school in the town, on his honor to return by bus to the detention center every day. At the graduation exercises, Katrina sat in one of the front rows.

Steve was released after almost three years at the center, but even then he experienced rejection. His mother, who had reappeared on the scene at the time of her son's notoriety, refused to have him live with her. His father had been remarried to a girl not much older than Steve. His sister was involved in a romance and had no interest in offering a home to a young brother. A downeast cousin ultimately accepted Steve into her home, and through her husband, Steve learned two trades.

I do not name these trades, as I have not used Steve's real name, for the reason that the boy has already paid for his crime by due process of law. And I don't want to identify him in any way, thus making trouble for him. This is despite Steve's own openness about his criminal record, which I agree with Katrina is indicative of his innate soundness and responsibility. He now works as a salesman, traveling the state of Maine, and his employer knows about the long-ago tragedy. Steve told him at the time he applied for the job—and the employer has been so pleased with Steve's work that when another employee came to him with a rumor of the killing, the tattler was fired.

After settling in his cousin's home and the new job,

Steve began attending church, mindful of Katrina's teachings, and it was there he met Meg and fell in love. They were married on Katrina's birthday and at this writing are expecting their first baby.

Steve tells his friends about Katrina—and about the Foster Grandparent Program. "When I was at the center," he says, "it cost the taxpayers ten thousand dollars a year to keep me there. But because of my foster grandmother I'm out of there. Probably a lot of other guys, too, because Katrina sends out love to them all. It's a crazy world when you get more love in jail than you get at home. I'm making good on my own, and I'll never in my whole life do anything to get sent back to a place like that again."

Steve is making it, and Katrina is puffed up with pride. "He is as much my child as are my own to me and so is his little wife."

Since Steve left the detention center, Katrina has worked with countless boys. Currently, her biggest worry is Owen, who got into trouble when he began skipping school. "Where was his mother?" complains Katrina. "Why wasn't she aware he wasn't going to school? Where *are* all the parents? They're split, they're living with lovers, and there's pot and booze in the homes. How can we expect these kids to turn out right? Owen, now, they've sent him back with his mother again. I hope she pays attention. I hope she gives him love."

Proud as she is of Steve, Katrina may be even prouder if Steve becomes the father of a daughter. It's not a positive decision, but the idea is being bounced around that if the baby is a girl she might be named Katrina.

ELIZABETH

The doctors told her, finally, that she had only six months to live. At the most. The uterine cancer, very probably contracted from radiation during the years when as a nurse she had done her own lab tests, had been killing her for some time, but now the final verdict was in. Six months.

If that's all the time I have, Elizabeth Mick told herself, I'm going to do something worthwhile with it. So she joined the Foster Grandparent Program in Brandon, Vermont.

In those days it was possible for a grandparent to choose a child, and Elizabeth chose Terry. If she had thought why, she might have answered it was because of his smile. The boy was eleven years old and blind and mute, but he had a smile that was spectacular because it was so genuine. She thought it remarkable that a little boy with so many disadvantages could smile at all.

Her interest deepened when she learned his story. Terry had been in the home for the mentally retarded since he was five years old. He had been two when his father walked away from the family—his wife, daughter, and blind son. For the next three years Terry's mother fought a good fight, trying in what turned out to be a vain attempt to take care of her children as well as earn a living. The only job she could find was work in a mill, and although she took it gladly, she almost collapsed under the strain of what to do about Terry while she was at work. He was not easy for others to handle; he was unhappy if away from his own home or his mother, and neighbors who volunteered to help by keeping him in their homes soon gave up, because he would cry and sometimes scream most of the day. Even without his insecurities, Terry was a difficult child to care for because of his blindness. His older sister adored him and worried about him excessively, but neither she nor her mother could find an answer to the pressing problem. And after fighting like a tiger for her cub, Terry's mother finally was able to place him in the local training school.

From the time he was six until he was eleven—years when most children are going to school to learn their ABCs—Terry lived in a world of noise made by other boys. The sighted ones, ranging from emotionally disturbed to profoundly retarded, played as roughly or more so than most boys, yelling at the top of their lungs. For Terry in his darkness, it was frightening to hear the screams and cries of the other boys, not knowing what was taking place and terrified that at any moment he might be jostled as they rushed past him or, worse, thrown to the floor.

When with his mother, he had learned nursery rhymes and had sung them. Terry loved music. At home he had a toy piano, and from the time he began crawling would go to where it was kept and hum while he plinked the keys with one finger.

Then everything had changed, and Terry no longer sang or spoke. His mother had been warned by the staff that he might change after admission to the home, and he did indeed. Part of the change might have been due to the

116

fact his mother was advised not to visit him for the first six months or so to give him an opportunity to adjust to his new surroundings. This did not work in the prescribed manner; it is very possible that the separation from his mother backfired seriously.

When foster grandmother Elizabeth Mick first saw Terry, he was eleven years old and sitting naked on the tile floor of the ward. The staff explained to her that the boy disliked all clothing and insisted on removing everything after they had dressed him—and that he apparently liked the soothing sensation given by cool tile on summer days.

Sitting on tile made sense to Elizabeth but nakedness did not. Nor the fact the boy was not toilet trained. There were things needing to be done here.

"I'll take that one," she said.

"He's blind," she was warned. "He's unteachable."

"I'll take him," she repeated.

Back in 1968, Elizabeth Mick was already stooped from old age, a fact she hated, because it made her seem even tinier than she actually was. She hadn't the vanity to consider that the stoop was more than made up for by her wondrously unlined skin, the halo of snow white hair, the bright and wise old eyes, and the Scottish brogue that charmed everyone she met. She had emigrated to the United States in her middle age; there was nothing to keep her in Scotland as never having married she was childless. "A maiden lady," she called herself.

She had been given six months more of life, and so at the end, she would finally have a child. Working with Terry each morning she told herself it would not be enough time. There was so much, so *much* to teach him. The staff's admonishment that the boy was unteachable fell on deaf ears.

First things first, she thought, and accomplished toilet training. Then came clothes. Every time he took off a garment she patiently put it back on. Terry responded; he undoubtedly felt the love emanating from this lady whose touch was so gentle, whose voice fascinated him. They were the touch and the sound of love, things he hadn't experienced other than from his mother and sister. The staff was nice and good to him, of course, but they seemed never to have time to stop and talk with him, to try to teach him anything. This lady, this grandma, became a light in his world of night.

She taught him to bathe himself, to brush his teeth. She taught him how to feed himself, patiently guiding the spoon and his hand to his mouth. She made him stand again. Terry fought this for some time, because standing meant he might be pushed to the floor by the other boys. As for walking, it hadn't occurred to him to try for many years. Elizabeth guided him along one wall of the dormitory, counting doors aloud as they went.

"You see, Terry, you can find your way by yourself."

In the evenings Elizabeth spent hours with a teacher who was blind, learning from her how to read Braille. When she had mastered the alphabet, she dug into her cupboard for a tin designed for six muffins and then went to the local general store to buy five tennis balls. She took these to the training school, and on the first morning she placed one tennis ball in the upper left corner of the muffin tin and guided Terry's hand over it.

"A," she said. "That is the letter A. Now we shall learn T and E and R and Y, Terry, and you will be able to read your name."

Members of the staff were gentle with her. "Elizabeth, it's such a good idea, dear, but Terry can't do it. He can't learn."

She straightened to the point where she was almost her full four feet and ten inches. "Don't tell me what he can't do!" she flared.

Any boy who had been taught nothing between the ages of five and eleven, she reasoned, had a double hurdle to overcome in order to learn now. She simply would not accept the professional prognosis of "unteachable."

The muffin tin and tennis balls were Elizabeth's own idea. So was the piano, after she had learned from the boy's mother that he had liked music. She bought a toy piano, and though she knew nothing of music herself, she was pleasantly surprised when Terry began to pick out tunes. Elizabeth had only to hum a song, and Terry unerringly played it back to her. The toy piano was his joy, and he was often playing it when she came to him in the morning. Obviously he had musical talent, all gone to waste so far. If she could just find a real piano for him, sit him down to it, and see what he could do with it.

The story of Elizabeth's final victory is a stunning one. You may wonder, as I did, that she could be so successful in teaching Terry so many things in a period of only six months. The fact is that in the end providence gave her an enormous dividend—Elizabeth did not die until she had worked with Terry for a total of eight years. When reminded of her illness, she always said, "I am too busy to die."

When she did, Terry soon adjusted to a new foster grandmother, Marian Kebrick, a former opera singer. Here was the talent Elizabeth had wished for (and the "supply for the demand" I keep writing about), someone skilled enough in music to teach Terry. Marian took him into church and sat him at the organ, and that beatific smile lighted his face as with one finger he made music resound throughout the building.

By now Terry was a fully grown young man who would soon be too old to stay at the training center and would go to live in a community home. Until then, Marian had a couple of years with him, and during that time she taught him to play the piano, beginning with "Chopsticks" and progressing to the point that he could play at church services.

A speech therapist told Marian, who is a fifteen-year veteran of the program, that she would not be able to teach

Terry to speak. He had not moved his lips in speech since leaving his mother's side at the age of five. As a friend of Elizabeth's, Marian possesses a similar starch, and she said to herself, we'll see about that.

She first taught him to hum. Then she taught him to say, "Ah," making him repeat the sound after her. One day he came to her and voluntarily said, "Ah." And before he was sent to live in a community home, Terry could recite "Peter Piper," the whole of it from start to finish. He has learned many words and can pronounce the names of everyone he meets.

Terry has perhaps reached the highest pinnacle he is physically and mentally able to attain, and his mother credits the care given by the staff and, most especially, the love given the boy by his two foster grandmothers.

"Before Elizabeth came to him," she says, "I would bring him home for a few days, and he just seemed not to care any more. He wouldn't speak. I couldn't reach him, and I had all these thoughts about my having failed, about how maybe I wasn't handling him the right way. Whenever I brought him home he seemed so tired—I think he was tired because he was frightened out there with all the noise and being blind.

"But after Elizabeth there was such a change. And Marian too. I play music for him now when he's home with me, and he remembers some tunes well enough to play them on his toy piano. He comes home now at least one weekend a month, and I have him on holidays too. We've taken him camping and fishing, and he loves it when he feels a fish tugging at his line. At home, if I steer him to the rocking chair and turn on music on the hi fi, he is contented, and all this has happened because of the Foster Grandparent Program."

This book is a monument to all the grandparents. For Elizabeth Mick, it is a posthumous accolade. Tiny Elizabeth was a truly heroic human being.

NELLE

W hen I first heard about Nelle Luckett I thought she might possibly be the most remarkable foster grandparent of the whole batch of 18,000. It was reported to me that Nelle didn't learn to swim until she was sixty-seven years old, that she is now eighty-six, and teaches blind children to swim.

That did it, of course; I had to know more about Nelle who quite apparently rated a place in this book.

I learned that by now she has celebrated her eighty-seventh birthday, that her hair shows no trace of gray and that "it won't as long as I can help it,"—this last accompanied by a wink.

Nelle appears to be twenty years younger than she is. She has a son sixty-two years old who is now retired, and the fact startles her whenever she thinks of it. She has ten great-grandchildren, the oldest of whom is now nineteen. Born in 1895, when Grover Cleveland was president, Nelle was raised on an old-fashioned farm in Illinois where she helped hand plow the acres behind a horse, fed the chickens, chopped wheat, and slopped the pigs. She moved to

St. Louis when she married at twenty-one and has lived in the same apartment there for the past fifty years.

She hates her name because "every horse and cow is named Nell. That's why I put an *e* on the end, to be different. They were talking on the radio every morning one week about some old horse named Nell, and I phoned them and told them my name and what I do up at the Y and that I was doggone sick and tired of hearing my name put to farm animals, and they took the joke off the air."

Nelle bore four children and lost two, and the survivors had college educations. She didn't go to work until her children left the nest, and when she did, the job took place in a swimming pool. Her choice of vocation is very probably responsible for the remarkable body she has for an octogenarian. Nelle is tall, with broad shoulders, a slim waist and hips, and what have been called in St. Louis "swinging legs."

Back on the farm Nelle had not been allowed to dip into the nearby creek because it was impossible to know where the sudden deep parts were—and certainly was not permitted to wade into the Ohio River with its tricky currents. So she grew up without knowing how to swim, and the lack bothered her for sixty-seven years. At that age she told her husband she'd decided to take swimming lessons, and when he replied he thought it was a good idea, Nelle took off for the local YMCA.

"It took me three weeks to get up the nerve to put my face in the water. Then one day the rest of the class were all down at the other end having fun, and suddenly I was so ashamed of myself huddling back at the corner of the shallow end that I said, Nelle, you're awful. I put my face in and swam to the deep end, and they all clapped. From the cheering you'd have thought I'd gone around the world."

It developed that Nelle was a natural swimmer. She passed exams and worked as a lifeguard at Y pools, and before her husband died in 1963 began teaching swimming to both adults and children. The jobs came in handy when she was widowed, and she then began teaching blind children. Ten years ago she joined the Foster Grandparent Program and was placed within the school system to help teach classroom work to emotionally disturbed children.

She still does that, but she ceased teaching the blind to swim two years after joining the FGP, when she was pushing eighty. "I figured I ought to stop because I was getting on in years. When you teach blind children to swim, their lives are entirely in your hands. I was afraid I might slip up some day and not notice a child in trouble, and so I stopped."

She did, however, put a light in the lives of hundreds of children who have learned to swim in the pool at the school for the blind. Teaching them has been a matter of implanting trust from the beginning.

"They have less fear than sighted children," says Nelle. "They can't see the water, know where the surface is, and once I got them to trust me it was easy. Because if I said you can do it, they believed me."

She taught all ages. ("The two-year-olds are easy.") First they sat at poolside and dangled their feet, then she turned them on their stomachs and had them kick in the water. Then came the part she herself had hated most— faces in the water. She made it easier for them; she held them in her arms and taught them to blow bubbles. When they could swim, she taught them to dive. From the diving board. They trusted Miss Nelle.

Some of her sighted students now play water polo. One won a state championship, and scores are earning money as lifeguards. As for the unsighted, they have a joy that would not have been possible without Nelle.

So that's what I learned about her. I kept hoping that I'd find out that somewhere along the way that Nelle had used her swimming ability for the good of the Foster Grandparent Program. But it turned out that the teaching of swimming has had nothing whatsoever to do with the ten years Nelle has worked with myriad children in the St. Louis schools, loving it at noon each weekday when they have come to her with a hug and a kiss and said, "Good-bye, Miss Nelle," for yet another day.

But somehow I feel she belongs in this book regardless. She is not only a foster grandmother, she is something else, is Miss Nelle.

LOUISE

In the case of Louise and Tommy it was a switch—he adopted her.

Louise Napier was a spry seventy-two when she joined the Foster Grandparent Program ten years ago at the East Mississippi State Hospital in Meridian. During the orientation process she and other foster grandparents were guided through the hospital and its grounds in order to become familiar with all its facilities. As Louise arrived each morning she noticed a teenage boy always on the scene, seemingly waiting. Later, he would follow the group everywhere. He was a handsome boy with deep blue eyes and a shock of dark hair, and one of the other foster grandmothers took a shine to him.

So it was that when Louise overheard the boy say to another youngster, "I know which one I want," she turned to congratulate the other woman but was suddenly confronted by the boy, who kissed her on the cheek and said, "Will you be my grandmom?"

Tommy's admittance to the hospital the previous year, when he was fourteen, had followed ten years of his having been shifted from one foster home to another. He had been diagnosed as a "moderate mental defective." He was unable to recognize even two- or three-letter words, and it was discovered he was unable to read or write; no one had attempted to educate him. In addition to his congenital mental problem, there had been a trauma that had left him with a speech defect. When Tommy was little more than three years old, he had watched his father murder his mother with a hatchet.

After Louise had been assigned as his foster grandmother for a month at the hospital, Tommy began saying he wanted to go home with her. When she reported this to friends and neighbors, they were horrified. They didn't understand how she had the courage to even enter the grounds of the "lunatic asylum," let alone even think of bringing a mental patient to her home—a mental patient who was a big and strong boy.

Fear never occurred to Louise. Tommy was a friendly, likable boy with a deep sadness in his face, and her pity for his situation endeared him to her the more. She asked for and received special permission to have him at her home on weekends, and thus began a loving relationship that no doubt will last as long as they both live.

From the beginning, Tommy told Louise that she reminded him of someone, and when Louise asked who, he pointed and said, "She's up there."

One morning in the kitchen she asked how he wanted his eggs cooked for breakfast, and he said he'd like anything but scrambled, because scrambled eggs were lumpy.

"Not *my* scrambled eggs," Louise said, and Tommy laughed.

"Why didn't God give you to me for a mama?"

Louise fought back sudden tears and said, "Well, he didn't give me to you, but let's think that he sent me to you."

The boy seemed satisfied with that and returned his attention to breakfast, but then he saw her tears and asked if she was crying.

"No," lied Louise, and the incident passed; but from then on he called her mama instead of grandma.

The third time she had him in her home, he had finished drying dishes for her and went into the living room to sit on the couch. "Mama, come sit beside me," he called to her. "I have something to tell you."

As women will, Louise continued putting dishes away in the cupboards, and he called to her to hurry. When she entered the room, Tommy patted the cushion next to him and said, "Sit close, mama. I need you to sit close to me."

Then he told her the story, in gruesome detail, of the murder of his mother by his father. Incredibly, he could remember the scene that had taken place when he was only three years old, and now it was obvious that the horror had stayed with him all those years in terrible clarity.

His father had struck his mother with the hatchet, and his mother had screamed and screamed, and the father had continued the attack, mutilating her sexually. As he spilled out the story, Tommy's voice was choked with tears, and Louise held him, her own face wet.

"But honey, how can you remember all that?"

"I was a little bitty kid, but I remember. Mama, I do remember. I was so scared, but I went over and grabbed my daddy's breeches leg, and there was blood all over him. He pushed me back, but the blood got all over me. Mama, I watched my mother die."

She held him and rocked him, and a bit later asked where his father was now.

"In prison. I hate him."

"You shouldn't," said Louise, summoning charity from deep within. "He's paying now for what he did."

"I hate him," Tommy repeated. The boy had no forgiveness. Months later they told Louise at the hospital that Tommy's father had died in jail and asked her to tell the boy.

"No," she said. "You people tell him."

Later he said to her, "Guess what. My daddy is dead." That was all. No grief, no relief, no emotional response. He never mentioned it again.

He evinced no interest in his siblings, a brother and

sister who, according to hospital records, existed. Louise once asked him if he'd like her to get in touch with his brother, and Tommy replied, "My brother is dead." He had blocked him out, and the brother might indeed have been dead for all the compassion he had for Tommy. The hospital felt the boy was well enough to live with family, but letters sent to the brother were entirely ignored until he returned one, having written across it "NOT INTERESTED."

Tommy seemed not to suffer from being abandoned by his siblings and soon adopted not only Louise as his own but her entire family as well. When she introduced him to her brother and sister-in-law, they immediately became his aunt and uncle. The family dog became Tommy's dog. The family youngsters in his own generation were referred to by him as his cousins. Another sister-in-law's husband became his father. When his new "daddy" died, Tommy was given his good blue suit, and although Tommy was much too big for it, it had been worn by the man he thought of as father, and he has it still.

When Louise first saw Tommy, he had been barefoot and was wearing a torn shirt. He had then been at the hospital one year and had behavioral problems, such as lack of grooming, and was sometimes a troublemaker among other residents. She bought him a new shirt and suggested that he dress himself decently. He ate too fast, shoveling food into his mouth. Louise taught him to sit up straight, how to hold a fork properly and told him to slow down. If Louise had told him to jump over the moon he would have tried.

She taught him how to count, how to tell time. He didn't know how to open a door; he opened doors by kicking them.

"Where I come from," Louise told him, "you don't push a door open like that. You open it with your hand like this—and then let ladies go through first."

He never forgot that, nor did he forget the lesson given him by a Navy officer who often visited the hospital to play games with the children. The man had taken Louise and Tommy shopping and afterward suggested they stop at his house on the way back for milk and cookies. While there he taught Tommy how to seat a person at table. The next time Louise took him to a restaurant, he stood beside her chair and then seated her as though he had done it all his life. "How'd I do, mama?"

Telling this, Louise wipes at her eyes and apologizes. "I'm sorry, I just can't help crying over that boy. He has become such a sweet person, so affectionate. In that way he's more like a little boy than a grown man—you walk past him and he'll grab you and give you a kiss. He keeps telling me 'Mama, I love you so much.'"

Tommy improved remarkably in meeting people. His behavior problems disappeared, and he became a pet at the hospital. It was Tommy who caught the girl patient trying to run away from the grounds and into traffic. It was Tommy who voluntarily helped blind Ernest to dress and then took him to church.

During the three years Louise worked with him at the hospital, he grew like a weed, ultimately topping six feet. The sadness disappeared from his face, as did the suggestion of mental retardation. His relationship with Louise and her family seemed to wipe away all indications to the point that unless someone knows him, they would never guess from Tommy's appearance that he has a mental deficiency.

When he turned eighteen, Tommy was removed from the Foster Grandparent Program, which at that time cared for children only under that age; and at the age of twenty-one, he was transferred to an adult residential mental retardation facility 200 miles away from Meridian. If anything, the bond between him and Louise strengthened when he was removed from the FGP, and since he has moved, Louise has visited him "every chance I get." That isn't often as she still works five days a week as foster grandmother to other children, and the 400-mile round trip is neither easy nor affordable. Regardless, she makes the drive at least one weekend a month.

"I just get my car parked up there, and he comes running like a jackrabbit, jumps in the car and says, 'Oh, mama, I'm so glad to see you!' When he first went up there, the staff thought I was his real mother because of his calling me mama. If I miss coming at least once a month, he calls me on the phone and says it's been too long a time."

That's something Tommy has learned to do—make a long-distance phone call. His mental deficiency remains; there are some things he learns one day but forgets the next. Dialing a phone is something he remembers, probably because it is the one way he can control contact with Louise. Last Christmas he was to spend the holiday at her home, and when she came down with a severe throat infection, her sister-in-law, Bernadine, phoned Tommy to tell him. Bernadine had no sooner hung up than Tommy was back on the phone, calling Louise.

"They gave him an emergency pass to come home early that Christmas," she says. "And if I'd had a maid around the house, she couldn't have done a better job. He kept telling me to sit down. He made the beds, he fixed my breakfasts, and did the dishes. He'd fix dinner when I told him how. One day he was down on his knees, and I asked what he was doing—he was scrubbing all the baseboards."

As a ward of the state where he now lives, Tommy is allowed to earn a small amount of money by keeping the parking area clean around the shopping center and by mowing the grass there. Tommy has been cautioned, and must remember, to adjust the power mower to "slow."

When he goes "home" to Louise's house on his birthday and all holidays, the minute greetings are over with, Tommy mows her lawn, cleans her car port, and washes her car. Then he runs over to Aunt Bernadine's for a cup of coffee and to play with Trixie, *his* dog. Last year Bernadine became a foster grandparent when she turned sixty; she has been long acquainted with the program because of Tommy "who comes and goes around our house as he pleases—he's like one of our own."

Bernadine has often taken Tommy for weekends, and she is disturbed when she thinks about the unalterable fact that he'll never be able to go out into the world. "I know that if he'd had the training early in life," avows Bernadine, "he could have accomplished something. Tommy is mechanically inclined. He can fix small motors and with training he could have made it."

It is the prognosis of doctors that Tommy will always be institutionalized, perhaps in a halfway house but always in a controlled environment. But Louise and Bernadine and their respective families hold eternal hope. As an example, a member of the church Tommy attends has taken an interest in him and is attempting to teach him how to read. He works with Tommy three days a week on his lunch hour, and recently Tommy brought some books home.

"Look, mama, watch me read." She looked over his shoulder as he slowly read an entire page aloud. This happened so recently that Louise hasn't yet had time to learn if he really knows how to read or if he had memorized the text.

"He's so smart in many ways, you see. I know that at church when we sing, he sings right along, his words coming out just a beat behind mine. So I don't know if he's looking at me out of the corner of his eye and copying me or if he already knows the words or whether he really can read a little bit. Anyway, I told him to learn how to write so he can write me a letter."

Inasmuch as Louise has suggested writing, it is probable Tommy will try to learn. He will do anything to please her. When eight years ago she suggested he try out for the Special Olympics, he not only tried out, he won in the local competition and was given a gold medal for his prowess in the fifty-yard dash. There was the usual applause from the grandstand, and as the ribbon was hung around his neck, Tommy bowed his head and then lifted it high, his arms thrust outward.

"Thank you," he said. "I want you all to know that I did that for my mama."

"THE CAPTAIN"

No one in Portland, Maine, can remember having seen Captain Donald Crandall bareheaded. They suspect he may even wear the jaunty sailor's hat to bed. He is a familiar sight on Portland's waterfront streets and has been for many years.

"The Captain," as he is known by perhaps half the population, grew up with the sea. He was born on Peaks Island in Casco Bay, off Portland. The grandson of a man who owned the Swampscot ferry, which plied its way between Peaks Island and the mainland, the Captain began his life aboard the ferry as a deckhand when he was thirteen. "I loved that boat. She was double ended, one hundred twenty-five feet. She was my home for ten years."

He was eighteen when his grandfather pronounced him mate of the *Swampscot* and twenty-one when he became the ferry's licensed captain. He says now, "I think the old man favored me over my brother. My brother was a good kid who always said yes sir, but I was a scrappy kid who yelled back at him when he yelled at me. We fought like hell, and he loved me because I was like him."

Typically, he walked off the *Swampscot* soon after being licensed, because he had met a renowned boat builder named Captain Ed Wallace and went up to the boat yard at Wiscasset to learn the trade. He "went head over heels into boat building" and married soon after, having been careful to determine that his bride was sufficiently enamored of the sea.

Today, at seventy-four, he still views as death any existence away from the sea, and his keen eye and weathered face join a rolling gait that surely marks the slightly built old man as a sailor of long experience.

The Captain is representative of a disappearing breed of men, those prideful craftsmen who can take brass and wood (he sneers at the mere mention of fiberglass) and mold them into a seagoing vehicle that can take a man around the world. During the thirties and forties he was director of a naval yard that constructed liberty launches, and ever since he has worked on fishing boats, ferries, and yachts.

Since 1978, when the Captain joined the Foster Grandparent Program, the sum of all his experience and training has been imparted to youths at Portland's Boys Training Center, where minor delinquents are confined. He teaches them how to build boats, repair them, launch them, sail them, fish from them, "loft" them, love them—and earn a living because of them.

In the beginning, he was assigned four boys as foster grandsons and put them to work on a derelict thirty-six-foot liberty launch donated to the project by the Sea Scouts. The Captain called the boat *The Opportunity* because he knew that's what she was to the boys—a chance to learn a trade that could get them jobs when they were released from the institution.

They had come there off the streets, having been arrested for stealing cars, setting fires, refusing to attend school, and most of them were addicted to alcohol and drugs. "I had some that just lived on dope," says the Captain. "It's their background, and the dope puts them there. When you get dope, you get personality change. They couldn't get their hands on anything while they were at the institution, but some were still wacky just the same. They'd come to the boat and to me in the morning, and they didn't know where the hell they were." The captain tucks a wad of tobacco into his cheek and chews contentedly. "I had one who would stand up in the bow of the boat and look into the sky at eight A.M., and he was still there, like a statue looking at the sky, at noon. What he was seeing I don't know."

Unless they are spaced out from drugs, these fourteen- to eighteen-year-olds under the Captain's tutelage have amazed officials at the center. Not one has tried to escape while on leave with the Captain, and despite the fact any one of them would make two of the little man, none has made a threatening gesture toward him.

The plain fact is that the youths are in love with the idea of what they can learn from the master. He offers them a sort of last bastion of romance and adventure. The West has been conquered, but there is still the challenge of the sea, and the sea will always be there with its siren song to young men. Youths who formerly refused to get out of bed in the morning suddenly rolled out at dawn and were at the dock warehouse by seven, an hour before the Captain showed up for his morning FGP stint. He extended those hours, working all day, because eight students comprised his limit in order to teach well, and the waiting list back at the center was growing every week. Kids were not only enthralled by the opportunity of learning an adventurous trade from a master craftsman—logic told them that here was a chance to learn skills that would assure them of work throughout their lives. And work meant the chance to kick bad habits and go straight.

The staff explained the opportunity to the boys, knowing the Captain's skills had given them a lever to deal with the kids. "Here's your shot," they told the young offenders. "You won't get another chance in your whole life to work with a guy that has built boats for fifty years. He will be your personal instructor, and you'll learn all about the sea. You'll learn a real job skill, and there are few places where a kid can go from zilch income to fifteen thousand. You can move yourself right out of poverty."

It gave them a weapon in more ways than one. They also told the kids, "We have a long line of you guys wanting to get into this program. You go and get spaced out or come in drunk, the Captain will tell us, and that's it for you. Plenty of guys want to take your place."

The Captain himself had other ideas, however. He allowed as how he'd rather not report infractions. "They got to know right away I wouldn't squeal on them, and this got me their respect."

That was an important first step. The next was the problem of how to discipline these young toughs—or would have been a problem for any man other than the Captain. "I just told 'em when they came aboard, I'm the boss of this boat. We'll get along fine, if you do what I ask you. I'm not gonna push you, but I want you to do what I tell you. Well, most of 'em do any damn thing I tell 'em to. When they don't, I just throw it back at 'em. Yell and holler and scream. And roll tobacco in their hair. They hate that."

The Captain does worse if he has to. His aim is deadly, and when truly roused the Captain can fire a projectile of tobacco juice with the accuracy of a missile. One of the more literary young prisoners thought up the nickname of Captain Hook and promptly got a squirt of tobacco.

"Don't like that," said the Captain in his best down-east style. "Quit it."

By this time he has had eighteen as students, including one girl. There was a small squabble about that—the bureaucracy said they wouldn't send girls, because girls wouldn't be able to do the work. But the Captain disagreed and gives the one he finally got high marks in his taciturn way when he says, "Makes a good carpenter." Prodded for more, he says, "Well, she got to know what she was doing when she cleaned a skeg and what to put into a pindle hole."

The first groups of four had the truly golden chance of beginning the refurbishing of a boat whose wood was rotting, its caulking splintered. Under the Captain's direction they made *The Opportunity* seaworthy within three months.

And then, with a boat they could trust, they went to work to clean up the harbor of Portland. This has become a rite of summer off the coast of Maine, particularly this past summer when the city of Portland celebrated its 350th anniversary. Boys from the detention center go out with the Captain in whatever craft is available to them with long, pointed poles.

"Any harbor gets dirty and this is bad, particularly when there's a storm," says the Captain. "Stuff floats just under the surface, and that's dangerous. Pilings break loose from piers, and these float vertically beneath the surface. What you do is, you spear the junk as if you were using a harpoon, then swing the pole back over your shoulder, give it a quick jerk, and the stuff will fall into the boat."

Funds for the materials needed to restore *The Opportunity* were provided by the Maritime Preservation Society of the National Trust for Historic Preservation. Since then the Captain and his crews have repaired many boats and therefore have little trouble finding something to work on. The project is well known in Portland and has the interest of its citizens, who cooperate when dock or warehouse space is needed. Interest in the program gives an extra dimension to the lawbreakers; citizens whose laws put the kids into jail or the youth center realize that these same young people are now helping to keep their harbor clean. Therefore, the erstwhile street youngsters get recognition and applause from the public.

On the rare mornings when there is no boat to work on, the Captain and the kids take out *The Opportunity* and set the two dozen lobster traps they have collected to be checked out the following morning for the catch, and in the afternoon they go to work cleaning the harbor waters.

The Captain is happiest when he has a sailboat at hand. "Anything but sail is horrible," he teases "and *The Opportunity* is motor, but you gotta take what you can get."

Of the eighteen, the average youth has worked a year and a half with the Captain. In general, they have learned a great deal about many power tools. In specific maritime subjects, they have learned maintenance, how to launch, navigation, rules of the road, weather, rope splicing, and knots. "When they finish this program," says the Captain, "they can go out and get a job on a boat. This isn't something just to keep kids busy. This teaches them a real job. The boat is a very physical, very tough, romantic job for a man. One kid now, Rick, he couldn't compete for a minimum wage job because he couldn't present himself right in an interview. But he learned how to make nets and a little about the sea, and he's working now as a fisherman, and if he stays with it can probably earn eighteen thousand a year. That kid couldn't have made it anywhere else.

"There's Scott. He's a nice boy, a good boy. He's a little slow upstairs. I'm hoping he can get into fishing. But Sam, he's one of the best. He's really got it in him to be a builder. He loves boats. I'm hoping he gets into a boat yard. If I had my own back, the one I used to own in Portland, I'd give that kid a job in a minute.

"And take Andrew." [The only subject on which the taciturn Captain turns loquacious is that of "his" kids in the program.] "Andrew was a terrible alcoholic, but he really wanted to learn boats, and he was the best I've ever had. He asked how to loft a boat—that's the way you start to build one. You lay it down on the floor, full size of the boat, laid right out in chalk and pencil on yellow building paper. Then you take all your patterns off the floor to stand up and then build your boat around them. That's what they call lofting, and it's quite a stunt. Got to be accurate. A tricky deal. Andrew loved that so much he hauled me off the street one day to tell him what to do to loft a sixteen-foot boat. Now that's small, but whatever the size you got to use the same technique. I'd tell him in the afternoon what his next moves were, and he'd stay right there until nine, ten o'clock at night. When I came in next morning, he'd have it down just the way I told him. He did it on his own, that son of a gun, and he lofted that boat just as pretty as you'd ever see. He's out now, sober and driving a taxi, waiting to come back on *The Opportunity*."

Many of the boys have joined the Captain and his wife for coffee and doughnuts on the mornings when the car picked up the boys first and the Captain last. They would troop upstairs to his apartment to share breakfast before swinging on out to the boat. The Crandalls know how tough these kids are, but even Mrs. Crandall hasn't had an uneasy moment in their company. When the Captain chided them for sloppy beards and long hair, they laughed, knowing his bark is worse than his bite. When "graduates" see him now on the streets of Portland, they "holler and screech" to get his attention.

Of the boys he has taught, the Captain figures all are straightened out. "Some more than others, but at least eight have come out just fine. A lot of drug addicts have kicked their habit, and a lot of them have got contracts for repairing things from the skills they've learned."

The Captain isn't finished, not by a long shot. He looks forward to the time when the program will be given a permanent work area. "If we had a big enough space, like a warehouse, we could begin building skiffs, small boats like that." And he wants a sea program big enough that he can train boys to be first mates. That's the sort of thing Andrew waits for—along with a dozen other kids who want to learn more from the master.

For the present, however, the Captain is filled with happiness in the assurance that as long as he can teach, these boys will carry on the skills of boat building. As long as one youth is taught, correctly, the skill will not die out. This is even more important to him than the benefits brought to him by the Foster Grandparent Program. By the time of his seventieth birthday, his life was beginning to be empty of purpose. "There's nothing worse," he says, "than not knowing what to do with yourself."

This past summer has kept him busier than men half his age. Eight boys in his class, the harbor to be constantly swept clean of debris, and the christening of the boat, which he did not allow until *The Opportunity* had been restored as nearly as possible to its original condition, down to the last brass screw. The swirl of events landed the Captain in an article carried by the local newspaper, and he even came to the attention of a writer for the *National Geographic* magazine who wanted to know if the Captain would be up to an interview.

Captain Crandall takes it all with the Yankee good sense and the Yankee humor that are most definitely part of the backbone of America. When someone teased him by asking how he handled his fame, the Captain shifted a wad of tobacco to the left and said, perfectly deadpan, "Well, they wanted me in Hollywood. Couldn't make it."

RUBY

It takes a special kind of woman to work with young girls who have been sexually molested. She should be a woman of a certain toughness, because she must endure hearing stories of overwhelming horror. She must understand street language and pretend not to be shocked by it, because in many cases it is the only language these girls know. And she must be a woman capable of giving unending love, because love in its truest sense is the only medicine able to cure the victims of these crimes.

Ruby Koenen is that kind of woman, and fortunately for the girls who have lived during the past ten years at the Trinity School in Ukiah, California, Ruby is a foster grandparent. It is as though she appeared on the scene in answer to the prayers of the staff of the Redwood Empire Foster Grandparent Program. The territory covered there in northern California is wine country, its vineyards stretching across the program's three counties. Most of it is rural, with moss green hills of breathtaking beauty spotted by crystal lakes. Distances are so great that some foster grandparents must travel fifty miles a day to work with the children, and so it has been difficult to find volunteers with such dedication.

On the other side of the coin, Ruby is a foster grandparent in answer to her *own* prayer. In the month following the day she found her husband, Peter, dead, a hammer still in his hand, in back of their trailer home in the vineyard, Ruby had lost twenty pounds. She could not face food and was literally wasting away. One day she looked at Peter's old leather chair and sank to her knees, burying her face in its seat.

"Dear God," she prayed. "Give me a reason to live, or let me die."

On the radio playing softly in the background, a voice said, at that very moment, "Listen, all you senior citizens out there . . ."

To this day Ruby says the message of the FGP was a miracle straight from God.

She needed the program perhaps even more than it needed her. She and Peter had lived most of their married life near Monterey Bay, where he worked as a mechanic on boat motors. Peter loved the sea and was happy on that spectacular coast, but he knew that Ruby fretted that she had to "get the winter clothes out of storage to live through the cold fogs of July and August"—that she definitely did not view Monterey as God's country. For her, the ideal place to live would be somewhere with hills, away from the sea.

So when Peter retired he said, "Now, Ruby, we'll go to your hills, and you can spend the rest of your life looking at them." They put their trailer in the middle of a vineyard near Ukiah, where Ruby glorified in the sunsets when the hills turned from green to pink to purple.

When he died, only three months after they moved north, she was helpless. Peter had been the type of husband who said, "I'm the man; I'll take care of the bills and do the worrying. You just look pretty and raise our boy."

He babied her so much that when she became a widow, Ruby didn't even understand a checking account. Without his guidance she went through all their cash—the whole $1,800—in one month. Friends down south near the Monterey Bay kept writing her to come home. Ruby said no. "This is where he wanted to leave me, and this is where I'm going to take my stand."

The first day she worked as a foster grandparent at the Redwood Valley School where she began with two boys, she ate her lunch, and it was the first meal to stay down since Peter's death. Says Ruby, "It seemed like when I was in the company of the kids, I could eat."

Her medical background stood her in good stead with the handicapped. Ruby had always wanted to be a nurse but never having gotten the hang of chemistry, had failed the exam and then did the next best thing and became a nurse's aide. That was at the Monterey Hospital, and they gave Ruby the job of the dying patients. "Nurses never want to do that," she says. "People know they're going, and they want somebody to pray with them or hold their hand. I did that all winter, but in summers I wanted to be outdoors so I worked in the orchid house of a floral nursery, and after all the dreary winter, I'd have the beauty around me."

At Redwood Valley she worked with three boys she has never lost track of. One had been born a normal baby, but someone had hurled him into a bathtub, and after that he'd had seizures. All three were abused kids, unwanted by their families, and Ruby worked well with that sort of problem; it was reminiscent of her own childhood. She'd never been abused, but there'd been a definite feeling she was unwanted. Her mother died at the age of twenty-eight, having given birth to seven children. One was stillborn, two others died at the same time as the mother in the flu epidemic. That left four girls, including four-year-old Ruby who, family legend had it, would have better pleased her father had she been a boy. The oldest sister took over the mother role at the age of seven. "I can remember that little thing standing over the old hot stove in San Joaquin Valley where our father worked in the oil fields," says Ruby. "By the time she was eight she could bake pies."

When her father married a second time, Ruby and her stepmother clashed from the beginning; the only adult she remembers with fondness from her childhood is her adored grandfather. When Ruby came running from the oil fields with her hair full of cockleburs, the old man would take out his knife and cut off chunks of hair. "This way it don't hurt as much as combin'," he'd say.

So Ruby could relate to the boys assigned to her. She was enraged when parents failed to show up after promising to visit, and she'd hold the weeping boy and rock with him until his tears dried up.

Ruby did such a good job at Redwood Valley that the psychologist at Trinity, the school for emotionally disturbed girls, began asking for her, and after five years Ruby surrendered and went to Trinity. Here she was called upon for service above and beyond, if duty such as holding a child so frightened that its entire body quivers is considered outside the normal realm of child care.

"Of *course* it takes a lot out of me," says Ruby. "Holding them is all you can do. At the beginning, at least. It's love. Just love. I don't know how it is, but something about being a grandma—they'll open up to me before they will to the staff. So I can help the staff understand what has gone on with the girls."

What has happened to them is sordid enough to make strong men cringe—small bodies scarred from burns, from knife wounds. Children as young as three with venereal disease. Parents never heard from because they do not care. And parents who ask that their daughters come home for a few days and then send them back totally out of control.

144

Home visits almost always end in disaster; from Trinity with its balanced meals and health rules, the girls go to homes where they have access to a gamut of drugs or, at the very least, eat meals laden with sugar and starch. Says Ruby, "Every time they come back it's hell for a week or two trying to get them straightened out again. But they have to try—if the girls weren't allowed to go home to parents who ask for them, there'd be no hope of their difficulties ever getting ironed out.

"I can have only two at a time, but I kind of wish I could take the whole bunch. We work with two until we figure we're at a dead end, that we've gone as far as we can go. If we're successful, the girls go on to a group home. They are called satellite homes, and six girls live in each one with a sort of house mother, where they learn to live like a family. After that, a lot of them can leave to make their own lives."

Ruby talks most often of her current two, one a girl of eleven, the other ten. Molly is the eleven-year-old. Her parents are drug addicts, and when Molly was three they put her out on the street and told her to "bring money home from men." If she came home without money they beat her, and stuck needles into her, all over her body.

Mary is ten, and her horror began with her stepfather. "It's very often a stepfather," says Ruby. "The girl tries to tell her mother about it, the mother goes into a rage, and beats the child. Women never want to believe it, and it's true so often. Mary's stepfather was finally caught in the act and"—here Ruby's lips curl with disgust—"they didn't even put him in jail. There are slick lawyers, you know. Guys who say things like, "don't let this poor little child testify, it'll only upset her."

Ruby says that of the seventy-six disturbed girls currently in Trinity School she estimates seventy have been sexually molested. Helping the girls recover from their fear of men is the most difficult and perhaps the most special

145

thing that Ruby does. It is a slow and careful process, sometimes beginning in conversation with male counselors at the school, but always with walks through town in Ruby's company. Ukiah is one of those friendly villages where everyone knows everyone else, and Ruby makes a point of stopping to chat with the mailman, the handyman, the neighbor raking his lawn—her arm around the child's shoulders as they talk. Afterward she'll say, "Now, Molly, there was a nice man. Don't you think so?"

After a while, following the talks with men about how to raise orchids—because everybody knows that Ruby Koenen is an orchid expert—the child herself will say, "Well, grandma, I guess there *are* some nice men."

Says Ruby, "They come to me at first like tight little buds, all closed up, and it's such a joy to watch them grow and mature and unfold. I have my two now where it's just wonderful. I've told them about my marriage to Peter, that it was a love affair all our lives, and try to make them understand that there is a beauty about physical love. You've got to be frank and truthful with them, because they're used to gutter talk. It's only after I get them straightened out, like my two now, that when they start talking dirty I tell them, 'Hey, I don't appreciate that sort of language. Knock if off—you're ladies now.' So by this time when they slip and say something crude, they put a hand over their mouth and say, 'Sorry, grandma.' No sir, I have no worries about my two."

In eight years Ruby has had many successes and, typical of her outspoken nature, doesn't mind saying so. "I've not had one failure, not one. None of my girls have ever gone on to the insane asylum."

The very first girl assigned to Ruby at Trinity was almost nine years old, and when she arrived the school psychologist called Ruby into his office. "Now, grandma," he said, "this one's for you. I don't know if we're going to keep her here. She probably won't make it. But it's your job to try. Take her and see what you can do."

And that's what Ruby did. The child was so filled with distress that she wrote on the walls of the bathroom, I HATE EVERYBODY—I HATE THE WORLD—I EVEN HATE GRANDMA.

Ruby's eyes sparkle, remembering. "Notice she wrote *even* grandma. That showed she liked me. It meant there was hope. Then I *really* started in on her."

Today, Ruby and that first girl to come under her wing are so close in their love for each other that the child, now approaching her teens, seldom makes a decision without consulting her foster grandmother.

The girls do not always come from lower socioeconomic homes. One is the granddaughter of a professor at a California university, but her mother was a drug addict and absolutely useless as a parent. When the child was brought to Trinity she refused to speak, and they decided she was a mute. She rejected all activities with the other girls; even when the rest went swimming, this girl would, according to Ruby, stand around like a wooden Indian. One morning Ruby tried again to break through the wall the girl had built around herself, and finally put hands on her hips and glared at the child.

"I'll tell you something," she said. "I'm not going to put in any more of my time on you! You can't talk, so you're not even worth my while."

The girl's face turned blood red and she shouted, "Dammit, grandma! You made me break my promise not to say anything!"

Ruby grinned. "Oh, you *can* talk, can't you?"

That girl went on to live at a group home and is now slated to leave Ukiah and live with her real grandmother, the professor.

Ruby has taught her girls how to crochet, how to sew on buttons, and hem their slacks—"the only one here who knows what a sewing machine is for"—and thanks to her, two girls now know how to play the organ.

When her day's work is done at Trinity, she goes to her

home on two acres, takes in the dog and the cats and closes the door. She knows it is best to shut it off, that if she forgets it all for the night she'll be able to work better with her girls the next day.

Ruby's home is something special. There's the trailer, and right next to it the barn sheltering a horse. There's an ancient beagle, a twelve-year-old rooster, three rabbits ("for pets, not for eating"), and five doves which Ruby keeps caged in her bedroom during the winters. She claims their cooing helps her to go to sleep. Her home is the kind of place she knows her girls would love, but there's a rule against taking them home with her.

She has her own grandchildren who visit, a boy and a girl. Ruby had wanted a brood of her own but had only one son. Peter built the barn close to the house specifically for their granddaughter's old mare so that in winter warm drinking water could be run into the drinking tub. Ruby's pets seem to thrive as well as do her girls; the mare died at thirty-four and was replaced by a spirited Arabian. These days, sixty-eight-year-old Ruby, who is all of four feet ten inches, tosses bales of hay in addition to feeding the smaller animals. "I have to have hard physical work, or I don't feel healthy."

Her grandson comes on weekends to help, and three other boys enter her life every weekend—the three whose foster grandmother she was eight years ago. They're all grown now; one is married and has a child of his own. When the phone rings on Sundays, Ruby is almost certain it'll be one of her boys, reporting his life and loves and job to the person who is responsible for his being on his own.

When the sun sets Ruby sits down to watch it send rays of color above the hills she refers to as her own. "I get my strength from them," she says. "It's like in the Bible, I will lift up mine eyes unto the hills from whence cometh my help."

Feeling whole and healthy, Ruby is beset by only two

questions. The lesser one is how she can afford to buy a small horse—"you know, one I could get on." The big one has arisen because she went to a local college and learned Spanish as well as completing a course in child psychology. Because of her studies and her list of successes with the girls at Trinity, she has been promoted. They want her to live in a satellite home and be house mother to the six girls living there.

This would be a definite promotion, which will give her a salaried job rather than the two-dollar-an-hour stipend from the FGP. The small horse might then be possible.

"But I just don't know," she says, raising her glance to the hills. "Sure it's a step up, and so I'll give it a try for maybe a couple of weeks. But if I can't cut the mustard— and by that I mean if I can't stand missing my two girls— I'm gonna beg them to let me go back to Trinity and be just a foster grandma again."

PAPA PEREZ

Joseph Perez didn't swear when his tire went flat that afternoon on Tampa's I-75 because he is a man of gentle nature. Nonetheless he was definitely unhappy; at the age of seventy-eight the spine is not always up to a tire change, particularly with traffic whizzing by in the rush hour. The day seemed all the more maddening when he discovered his spare tire was also flat.

Wilting in the summer heat, he took off his hat and ran a sleeve across his forehead. When he looked up he saw that a pickup truck had stopped in the emergency lane and was backing up to his car. Two strapping black boys jumped out, and one hailed him.

"Papa Perez! How you doin'? What's wrong?"

The boy had to be six foot six and weighed well over 200 pounds, and Perez peered, trying to place him.

The boy laughed, even white teeth gleaming in his dark face. "You don't remember me, do you? Why, Papa, I'm the one who never wanted to do anything, remember? And you kept giving me the toughest jobs until I finally learned. Hey man, this here's my brother."

Papa Perez shook hands with the brother and recognized Rocky—not easily, because a dozen years had passed and Rocky was a foot taller.

As the boys removed the bad tire, Rocky told Papa Perez that he'd married and had a baby and that he'd joined the army. Half an hour after they threw the faulty tire and the spare into the truck and sped off to have repairs made, they were back. Rocky wouldn't allow Papa Perez to lift a finger, and when the car was again ready to roll, the old man asked how much he owed the boys.

Rocky looked at him in mock disgust. "You puttin' me on? Papa, that was for *you!*"

Papa Perez has been a foster grandfather for thirteen years now, and this sort of thing often happens to him— chance meetings with young men who at first sight seem to be strangers. The best part of the meetings is the unfailing discovery that the grown boys are an improvement over the children Papa knew at the Seffner Juvenile Home.

There was Ed, as tough a thirteen-year-old as can be imagined. Ed was a loner, unfriendly with everyone including his peers, often violent, and held hate in his heart for the world. The first time he showed up at Seffner, Papa Perez worked with him for three weeks before the boy was released; and two months later Ed was back again, arrested for breaking and entering. Over a period of three years Ed was repeatedly sent back, a catalyst in the institution, always starting fights and often being put in solitary for his offenses.

Papa Perez was always there to work with him, and little by little, responding to the old man's quiet interest, Ed told his story. He had never known his father, his mother was constantly drunk, and his oldest brother was in prison. He had two other brothers and a sister, and he told Papa, "Nobody cares nothin' about us." It didn't bother Ed in the least that a brother was in jail; jail was par for the course and where he himself was heading. His mother did matter; whether or not Ed realized it, he was deeply disturbed that he had had no sign of love from her.

"You got to forgive her," Papa told him. "People have problems, and sometimes they drink to forget those problems. You got to try to love your mama."

Ed responded with an epithet. "I gotta get outa there."

"No, son, you stay home 'cause you're a minor, and if you run away they'll only put you back here again. You've got to make the best of it for now."

When Ed was sixteen, Papa told him he was getting big enough to join the service. "You finish school and join the military and make a man of yourself."

After that, Ed didn't come back. And years later, as Papa Perez and his wife were sitting down to supper one night, there was a knock at the door. Ed stood there, a husky giant in an Air Force uniform. Papa went through the memory search once more, finally recognized Ed from his voice, and slapped him on the shoulder. "My gosh, you were nothing but a little runt last time I saw you!"

Ed stayed for supper and said he was studying engineering and soon would be shipped to California. He hadn't wanted to leave before seeing Papa. That Christmas Papa received a card and a gift from Ed, and that was the last he heard of him. Papa's eyes mist up a bit when he talks about Ed; despite the passage of time he still feels empathy for the boy and the home life forced on him. "Ed grew up in the streets. He had a tattoo on one arm, the signature of the gang he belonged to. Those kids have to belong to gangs—if they don't, they won't survive. It's a form of blackmail—join or you'll be sorry."

Ed was only one of the incarcerated boys who taught Papa the evil of the street gangs, and so when his own son joined one, Papa's back stiffened. "I don't like the company you're keeping."

"They're my friends, and I'm sticking with them."

"They're not your friends, son. I'm your only friend, the one that will stick to you, do anything for you."

"I'll see the guys whether you like it or not."

"Then I'm going to have to beat you up."

His son stared. This was not like his gentle father, the man who grieved for two dead sons and adored his five daughters.

"You do and I'll turn you in to the cops."

Papa Perez got out of his chair and went into action, and when his son finally picked himself up off the floor, Papa said, "Now you go call the police, and they'll put you up in front of a judge, and the same thing's going to happen to you—you're gonna lose."

Papa's son never went back to the gang. Not long ago Papa had dinner at his son's house, and after the children had left the table and the men were lingering over coffee, the son said, "Remember the time you gave me a shiner and beat me up?"

"I sure do, and I'm sorry about it."

"Well, I'm not. I'm glad you did it. You opened my eyes—you showed me that you loved me. Now that I have my own kids, dad, I can understand. And I thank you."

Papa Perez seems to have automatic influence with the youngsters who come under his wing. Perhaps it's because of his love for all children; he most certainly is accustomed to having them around. He had no brothers or sisters until he was ten years old, and then they began coming, three in all. Papa was babysitter for them for eight years and then got married when he was eighteen. By the time he was twenty-two, he had three of his own. He lost a son in infancy and another son in the Korean conflict, but the surviving son and five daughters have given him a baker's dozen of grandchildren. Those don't seem enough—Papa says, "If I didn't have the foster grandchildren to see every day, I'd go crazy."

When Papa Perez served for the FGP at the detention home, the staff advised him not to take the boys home or allow them to visit. "They're too much for you, Papa. They might rough you up. You'll see, one of these days one of them is going to jump you."

None ever did. There is still a stream of former grandsons stopping by. They pick grapes from the vine in back of his house or berries from the mulberry trees. They come by hoping they'll be invited to stay for a meal, because Papa loves to cook and proudly labels himself a gourmet chef.

Currently, the program has assigned him to a home for retarded children. There he works with them in a greenhouse, teaching them how to plant flowers and vegetables, the cultivating of which is just another of Papa's many talents. While he has finished with work at the detention home, at least for now, he has the satisfaction of knowing that while there he set many of the boys on the right road.

There was Ramon, the Puerto Rican. Ramon was a quiet boy and everyone liked him; he was at the home only because he was a runaway. The institution was ready to release him, but Ramon would not leave. One rainy day Papa was watching television with a black boy on one side of him and Ramon on the other. Papa put an arm around each boy, and when the black boy fell asleep, Ramon whispered to Papa, "I'll tell you why I don't go home. Here I get up in the morning and eat and go to school and have friends and people love me. I have a nice bed to sleep in. At home we never have breakfast, and we sleep on the floor. And you see, Papa, what you are doing now, putting your arm around me? My daddy never does that to me."

"Is there anybody you love?" Papa asked him.

"You. And my grandmother, my daddy's mama. She's a nice lady. I wish I could live with her."

Papa spoke to a counselor who set legal wheels in motion. The grandmother was overjoyed to have Ramon given to her; she said he had always been her favorite grandchild. Eight months later, Papa was walking through the parking lot of a supermarket on a Sunday morning when he was hailed by Ramon.

The boy, dressed to the nines in a jacket and tie, was sitting in the back of a pickup truck. He told Papa he was attending school in the mornings and working in the afternoons for his uncle who was in the construction business. "He's in the market now, and I'm protecting all this stuff in the truck for him. And Papa," Ramon said, "I sure do like it where I am now."

Another happy ending engineered by Papa Perez was the case of Luis and his brother Angel. Their mother was a drug addict who spent every cent of the child support sent her by the children's father to sustain her habit. She was gone from the home for days at a time. Papa looked into the case and learned the father had a trucking business in Ohio and was a responsible man.

"How'd you like to go live with your daddy?" he asked the boys.

"Him? He's a no good. He don't care nothing about us."

"How do you know that?"

"That's what mama says."

Of course Papa got busy and talked to counselors, who wrote the father. The father said he'd be happy to have his sons, that his business would be theirs one day. And so the boys were sent up north to Ohio, and one more notch was added to Papa Perez's many successes.

In the thirteen years Papa has been a foster grandparent, he has served his grandchildren in a wide variety of ways, so it is difficult for him to pinpoint his favorite memory. "But the time I was most honored," he says, "is I guess the day in church when I gave away the bride. That girl had got her life all straightened out and said she wanted me to put her on the road to living happily ever after. Taking her down the aisle to the altar was a pleasure I'll never forget."

JOE

S ally was a gleam of happiness in his old age. In his seventies, Joe Cashin had been divorced for more years than he could remember, and one of the saddest things about it was that he had not been permitted to watch his own grandchildren grow up. For a man alone, it had been a bleak existence, until he became a foster grandparent at the state hospital in Faribault, Minnesota.

He chose her himself, a tiny blonde thing in a wheelchair, so small that she belied her eight years.

"She looks about four," Joe said to the project director. "Can she walk?"

The answer was no. Sally's spine was lacking in strength, and she could barely stand.

Joe grimaced. "I know all about that," he said. Doctors had been at him for years to have surgery in the lumbar region of his spine. For Joe, it was agony to lean over.

One morning before he wheeled her outside for their daily stroll, Joe took from his pocket a small rubber doll and fastened it to the inside of the tray fitted to the little girl's stroller. When she moved forward against the toy, it

156

made a squeaking sound that delighted her. She began the habit of rocking back and forth in order to create the sound, and within a year the doctors discovered the muscles of her back had strengthened to an almost miraculous degree.

Joe beamed at the good news. Now could he teach Sally to walk? They said he could try, but they doubted he'd be successful.

Then began his patient (and painful) attempts to make the little girl take steps. To do this, he stood her behind her wheelchair and supported her while slowly moving the chair forward. She was so tiny that her head did not show above the height of the wheelchair, and when Joe leaned forward to help her, the torment showed in his face. The staff noticed and questioned the wisdom of his aggravating his back. He really ought to have the recommended surgery, they said.

"Then I couldn't be with her for a lot of weeks," said Joe. "Don't stop me. You know what this child means to me. She makes my days shine."

And so Sally eventually learned to walk, by herself, without the support of the wheelchair or help from Joe. He said the day she took her first step alone was the proudest day of his life.

When Joe was eighty, Sally died. The heart that had barely sustained her for eleven years ceased beating, and Joe's grief was a sorrowful thing to see. Her body was sent out west to her parents who wanted her to be buried in their town. With her went the little rubber doll. The parents knew it had given their daughter happiness and asked that it be sent with her so that they could put it in her coffin.

Joe finally had corrective surgery on his spine, but he never could bring himself to choose a second foster grandchild. He was sorry, he said, but his little girl could never be replaced.

"COOKS"

A nother nickname for a foster grandmother, and this time there's no explanation. Ruth Chavez says the monicker began when she was so young that she cannot recall its origin. Frankly, I'm relieved, because there is another Ruth in this book, and so a nickname will lend distinction.

Ruth Chavez, or Cooks, has worked all her adult life—in factories and as a maid in hospitals—and now at sixty-three she says, "It took me all these years to find a job I liked."

The Foster Grandparent Program provided her with this almost two years ago when she became foster grandmother to one-year-old David. The baby filled a need she had carried many years, the yearning for more children. Married when she was a young girl, Cooks told her husband she wanted ten children.

"No," he said. "We will have only two."

In the way of Mexican-Americans of her generation, Cooks surrendered without an argument. The man was the boss, and that was that. She bore a son and a daughter and followed Chavez where his work took him; from the open sky of her native and beloved Colorado to the city of San Francisco where "everything goes up instead of out" and to

158

Salt Lake City where, she says with a slight sniff of disdain, "It's even more crowded."

She was grateful when they returned to Pueblo in the foothills of the Rocky Mountains, where most of the people knew what you were talking about when you discussed livestock and farming. There she enjoyed the five grandchildren provided by her son and daughter. But they weren't enough; Cooks still longed to have children around her house, and babies in particular. When her husband died six years ago, she continued to work, this time doing housework for a woman many years her senior who became a friend as well as an employer and in 1980 told Cooks about the FGP.

Cooks was accepted immediately. By that time the program in Colorado had changed to the point where, depending upon need, a grandparent didn't always have two children. In Pueblo they needed grandparents to serve as backups in the area's foster homes, and Cooks was assigned to David. He was her one and only, hers alone for four hours each day.

The baby had been labeled as retarded by the doctors and placed, months earlier, in a foster home that sheltered four other retarded young children. Cooks took one look at David and said to herself, this baby is not retarded. Although she'd had no personal experience with the retarded, she loved all children, so much so that she always stopped on the street or in the parks to exclaim over them, to talk with their mothers. With David, she noticed immediately that his eyes did not have the shifting gaze of the mentally retarded; David's eyes were strong and bright brown, sparkling in the little face that was half Mexican and half black.

When he was slated to undergo infant-stimulation therapy, Cooks was asked to take him for the tests, and there she said, "This child is not retarded. Look at his eyes. They don't turn in at all."

When she had protested previously, no one had paid attention to her. This time they argued with her, and

Cooks argued right back. "He's just picked up patterns from the retarded children he's been living with," she said. It ended the same way—the subject was dropped.

Cooks picked David up each morning at the foster home where it seemed he was almost shoved out the door. Cooks was never asked to come in, but the message that she was unwelcome did not deter her or put a dent in her enthusiasm. If anything, it strengthened her love for this year-old baby who had not said a word, had not taken a step, and was so frightened ("spooked" says Cooks in the manner of people who live in horse country) that he hid his face at the approach of a stranger. He drooled and at first kept his small fist in his mouth. But Cooks gently took it out and wiped his chin, telling herself this sort of nonsense was only in imitation of the other babies at the foster home. Each day she played with him at the nursery where he cried when she left him to have lunch. Some days she took him to her own home to cuddle and talk to him. She talked to him constantly. Living alone, she would prattle to him about her household tasks, whatever it was she was doing. She took David through the park in a stroller, telling him about the sky, the trees, the birds, the flowers. No matter that he couldn't understand; he was her little friend, and that's the way she talked to him.

Within three months David was talking back to her. In point of fact, he talked so much that she sometimes thought he would never stop. And in those three months he had also progressed from standing to walking; David walked so well that his normal gait was almost a run.

Cooks was unaware that anyone was noticing what she did or how David was acting—until the day a psychologist told her, "Mrs. Chavez, you have done a great deal for David. He is a totally different baby since you've been caring for him."

"I don't know how I did it," she said. "I only went to fifth grade in school, but I sure knew he wasn't retarded."

"You were right. He is totally normal, and he will be put up for adoption."

This was good news and bad news. Cooks was overjoyed for the baby, but it meant that she would lose him as a foster grandchild.

They gave her Vernon then, probably because no one else had the patience he required. Vernon had been born of an alcoholic mother and he cried endlessly. Every waking moment the baby howled and screeched as do so many infants who developed within the uterus of a heavy drinker.

Cooks rocked him and sang to him and sometimes, to keep her sanity, had to hold her ears. But somehow she stayed with Vernon and withstood his caterwauling four hours every morning. "Somebody had to help him," she says simply. And she did, for Vernon has completely ceased his crying and is being put up for adoption. Again, Cooks is losing a baby she loves but is already adamant that Justin, the mentally retarded boy about to be assigned to her, is *not* retarded. "It's the same as David," she says. "His eyes are so bright and alive." Grandma Chavez does not give up easily—in life or on love. She pines for David and has engineered a small espionage system whereby, through other foster grandparents, she has occasional news of David, now almost three years old. Said one foster grandfather, "That boy doesn't shut up for a minute!"

Cooks laughed and said, "I know."

She feels good about David because he has been adopted by a warm and loving couple who had a baby girl soon after adopting David. Cooks has met the mother and says she is a beautiful person. It has never been suggested that Cooks stop by to visit David, but she will very probably do it regardless.

"I'll drive by his house in a year or two. And if I see him outdoors, I'm going to get out of the car and hug and kiss him. Even if he doesn't know who I am."

BERTHA LEE BAILEY
1891–1976

H er very name had a lilt to it, as did Bertha herself. Music was a large part of her life; she studied it at two colleges and a conservatory and taught it in Indiana. For a time, she graced the Broadway stage in the 1927 original production of *Show Boat*.

For those who remember her as a foster grandmother at the Vineland State School in New Jersey—a crippled woman of more than fourscore years who hobbled rather than walked—it is difficult to believe that their beloved old Bertha once lifted her contralto voice in song at the Princess theater as part of the all-black cast of Jerome Kern's *Show Boat*. Bertha herself seldom referred to that glamorous era of her life. It was a typical restraint, as she regarded service to others as the crowning achievement of life.

She combined her love of music with her dedication to education, and the result of the merger was a lifetime career of enriching the lives of others, most of them children. To do this, Bertha Bailey had to have an education, not an easy thing for a black, and a black woman at that, in an era when education was limited in many areas to black

162

women. If Bertha was not permitted enrollment in an institute of learning she preferred, she simply went elsewhere until she found a college where she was accepted.

Given the prejudice she had to overcome, the list of Bertha's accomplishments is a stunning one. A teacher's certificate was awarded at Indiana State Normal School, after which she taught in two Indiana schools. Then followed a course called Public School Music at Northwestern University, after which she was supervisor of music in the public schools of two Indiana cities. She returned to college to earn her Bachelor of Science degree in education at Tuskegee Institute, then returned to her favorite combination when she discovered a course on religious education and humanology at Buffalo University. While in Buffalo, she was a student of voice at the Buffalo Conservatory.

Marriage to James Bailey brought a halt to Bertha's continuing education but not to her activities. She got around in those days, to put it mildly, and her quest for projects was unrelenting. While in Port Norris, New Jersey, she visited a dreary suburb known as Shell Pile because its residents earned a living by opening oysters. The people were shockingly poor and uneducated, and within months Bertha had established a community center for children during the day and adults in the evenings. Noting the rigid diet of fish and rice, Bertha organized the grownups to raise vegetables and thus supplement their diet. She taught sewing and cooking and, of course, music. Some of the men at the center formed a quartet and appeared on the Major Bowes radio show, thus fulfilling Bertha's special love of choir and choral singing. Later, living in Alabama, she became a freshman counselor at Alabama State Teachers College and ultimately had three of her own radio shows.

But for Bertha—and this is according to her, as you will learn at the end of this story—life really began in 1968 when she was seventy-seven years old. At that point she

163

had suffered many years from arthritis and could walk only with the aid of two canes; sometimes she even found a walker necessary.

On the day she applied to become a foster grandparent, she parked her car at the Vineland State School, left her canes in the back seat, and walked unsupported to the director's office. Then a widow for four years, Bertha had yearned to join the program since first hearing of it and was not about to kill off her chances by appearing to be crippled. Furthermore, she told herself, if she were lucky enough to be accepted, she wouldn't want the children to think her weak because she needed the canes.

She never used them again, at least not within sight of anyone at the school, its staff, or children.

With the advent of grandma Bertha, the program at Vineland took on an added sparkle. "She was remarkable, a takeover kind of person," recalls the director, "and almost immediately she got into a leadership capacity here."

Before her death eight years later, Bertha traveled all over the state to laud the program. She capped her testimonials when she appeared before Senator Alan Cranston's Committee on Human Resources and Child Development to explain the Foster Grandparent Program.

"She was the major attraction," recalls the director. "People were captivated by her. She was extremely articulate and not at all nervous, even when speaking before the committee. In a crowded elevator in the Senate building, someone asked her how long she expected to be around, meaning Washington, and when she said, "'Oh, at least another three or four years,' everybody broke up. Bertha was quite realistic about death. She wasn't intimidated by it."

It was part of her inherent dignity, an inner quality further enhanced by the proud way she held her head and the upswept hair, done in careful braids that framed fine eyes and patrician features describing kindness and intelligence.

The Foster Grandparent Program gave Bertha her first crack at working with mentally retarded children, and she loved it, gloried in it. With her teaching experience she introduced many innovative ways to help the youngsters.

In her eight years with the program, she worked in the main with two girls, Gladys and Peg. Gladys was the more difficult of the pair, an extremely hostile child without speech who had never known how to love or to accept love. At the time Bertha was assigned to her, Gladys spent her waking hours doing absolutely nothing, simply staring into space during the periods she wasn't having tantrums. She was often so violent that Bertha chose to sit with a chair between her and the child. She talked to her constantly, looking for a reaction. She brought a mirror and held it in front of the youngster's face. "See, this is Gladys. Gladys is your name. Smile at Gladys." The initial victory came on the morning the child looked into the mirror and said, quite clearly, "Gladys." Ultimately, the girl greeted her foster grandmother with, "Good morning. I am Gladys." She became an affectionate, outgoing child, apparently happy in her limited world because she often laughed and nestled close to Bertha.

Peg made more progress. Bertha taught her shapes and colors and communication skills, initiating word banks and color banks. Peg learned to read at kindergarten level, to recognize traffic signals, and attained a vocabulary of fifty words. On payday, Bertha took Peg with her to the bank, where the child proudly handed the endorsed check to the teller and received in exchange the cash representing Bertha's stipend. Bertha took Peg with her when she was asked to explain the Foster Grandparent Program to sundry organizations and women's clubs. She would describe Peg's disabilities when she'd first been assigned the child and then go through a drill with Peg to illustrate recent accomplishments.

Bertha was proud, yes, but she was also humble.

Acutely aware of her crippled condition, she tried to hide her gnarled hands and to disguise the pain suffered when she walked. She once wrote a letter of apology to the program director: "I do not wish to embarrass you because of my condition, nor to be an object of pity. Here I am, hobbling around, and I am concerned that I may be an embarrassment to you. If this is true, please let me know, and I shall resign with complete understanding."

Another letter, written six months before her death from a blood disease, was touching enough to bring tears to the eyes of those who read it. In part, Bertha wrote, "I am facing a serious problem by now, because I must live alone. As you know, I have a fine son, a foster son, a wonderful daughter-in-law, four grandchildren and five great-grandchildren, all living in their own homes. They have offered me a home, but I do not wish to accept. Would it be possible for me to have room and board on the Vineland State campus? I want to work with the retarded as long as I can get results from my efforts. I love them so. I have hospital insurance and my burial plot is paid for, so you see, I would not be a burden to the state or the staff. I should like to be of use in addition to being a foster grandparent in the afternoons. I could work mornings, maybe feeding residents or as desk relief. Nor would I mind working evenings. I plan to sell my house so that I could help with my expenses at the school. I'm hoping you might find a space for me on campus. I'd be most grateful if you would consider this proposal. Bertha L. Bailey, FG."

With deep regret, the staff had to turn down her plea; a state institution couldn't allow residents other than those referred by medical personnel

But once Bertha had died, they did something that would have perhaps embarrassed her but most certainly would have pleased her. They set up an annual award in her name, a plaque in the shape of the state of New Jersey. The announcement read:

BERTHA LEE BAILEY MEMORIAL AWARD

This award is presented in memory of Bertha Lee Bailey, who served with the Foster Grandparent Program at Vineland State School from February 1968 until her death on April 14, 1976.

Mrs. Bailey contributed much to our program during her years of service above and beyond the normal functions of the position. She spread the name and reputation of the New Jersey Foster Grandparent Program far beyond the boundaries of our State. This contribution is a culmination of her life of service to her community and fellow man wherever she resided.

We intend to present this Award annually to a person who has rendered outstanding service to the Foster Grandparent Program.

The award caps the achievements of Bertha's last years and confirms one of her favorite sayings: "in life, all the sugar is at the bottom of the cup."

ELFREDA

For the past five years she's been in a nursing home and now at eighty-six is confined to a wheelchair because of the deterioration of her spine. Elfreda Brandt doesn't grumble about pain, but she does fret about having had to leave the Foster Grandparent Program.

After all, in 1975 she had been the very first foster grandparent in Fort Wayne and had even been given a plaque by Indiana's governor for her ten years of service. And she had sat in the Blue Room of the White House in 1976 when all the "ten-year" grandparents were invited there. And then this darned thing with her spine, not being able to be with "her" grandchildren.

The FGP began for Elfreda after she had worked more than twenty years as traffic manager for a local firm and was sick and tired of working over a typewriter. She felt strongly that the most wonderful thing that could happen in her later years would be the opportunity "to do something for somebody who's hard up or sick or needs some sort of help." She was already past sixty when she read about the Foster Grandparent Program in the newspaper, applied, and was immediately accepted.

Before we get into the story of Elfreda and Joey, I think I might apologize for overworking the word "miracle" in this book, but there is no other word I know of that aptly describes so many happenings within the FGP. I say that Elfreda's work with Joey was a miracle, and perhaps you will agree with me.

When she first saw him, Joey was two weeks old, a tiny black thing so ill he couldn't move, not even his fingers. "He didn't look human, he was so thin and long and slinky," says Elfreda now. "It scared people just to look at him, and I was no exception. The staff had asked me to take him, and I had to leave the room and come back in again a couple of times so I could gather some strength out in the hall."

Nobody wanted this little thing who'd been brought to the county children's home, and doctors didn't wonder at the lack of interest. They said that Joey couldn't possibly live, that he would probably die any day now. Elfreda shrugged at the doctors' pronouncements. Joey certainly didn't look very promising, lying there inert with his eyes tight shut. But I can try, she told herself.

Each day when she left the children's home, a doctor or nurse would say, "Well, Mrs. Brandt, I guess today is Joey's last day. You'd better prepare yourself." But the next morning Joey was always there, still crying at the top of his lungs. The baby had reason to cry: he had been born with malnutrition that threatened his life even before birth. Joey's mother was a prostitute working in the poorer part of town, and when there was no money for food, she had scrounged through trash containers, eating anything that came to hand. It was not a diet to produce a healthy baby.

Each morning Elfreda arrived at the home with fear gripping her heart, then smiled when she looked into the room. Joey wasn't dead yet! She learned how to exercise his limbs to improve muscle tone and, it was hoped, to correct the bowed back. Soon he began to move in his crib.

Then he was able to hold his bottle. Later, there was a day when he sat up, unsupported by Elfreda's hands.

She worked with him on exercises in the mornings, and after lunch she went back to the home and stayed with him for more hours than were required for her stipend. "That was all right with me because I was doing something good, something for Joey."

Once she had succeeded in getting him to sit up, she spent most of her hours with him in attempting to teach him to crawl. Elfreda was seventy years old, but that didn't stop her from getting down on her hands and knees.

"Look, Joey, I'm crawling. Now, you crawl."

The baby only stared at her. She put one of his knees on the floor and gave him a little push. Then the other. Back to the first. "Now, Joey, watch me," and she would push one of her own knees and then the other. This had gone on for many weeks when one day she put him on the floor, got on her hands and knees alongside him and said, "Come on, Joey, you and me together."

And he crawled.

"He crawled eleven crawls!" says Elfreda now. "I rushed into the living room of the home and yelled 'Joey crawled! Joey crawled!' You might think I'd found gold or something, I was so excited!"

In the corner of that room there was an old armchair, and in the afternoons at nap time, Elfreda took the little boy there and said, "Come on, Joey, we're going to have a love-in." Joey didn't talk and never learned how, but he understood what Elfreda said, and he would laugh and snuggle close to her; this white woman was, literally, the love of his life.

She says, "There's a touch you give people that tells them you love them. It's nothing secret; it's just that you put your mind and your heart in the touch, and they recognize that feel of love. It's easy to do."

In the warmth of her love, Joey burgeoned into an extraordinarily handsome little boy. His brown skin shone with health, his face filled out to a perfect oval, his big brown eyes sparkled under long lashes. Gone were the anxious mornings when Elfreda had peered into his room, terrified that Joey's bed would be empty, that he had died during the night.

Now she taught him to stand. The exercises had strengthened and straightened his spine to the point where she was certain she could teach him to walk. And she did; by the time he was three he was walking quite well.

Elfreda insisted he was more normal mentally than the doctors had said. "We had this little two-seater swing, you know, the kind they have in gardens with the seats facing each other. One day after lunch I went into the living room, and there was my Joey, one foot on one seat and one on the other, making that swing go like mad. I was afraid he'd kill himself, but he stopped right away when I asked him to. You can't tell me that boy was so mentally retarded."

She bought him clothes and toys. She taught him to roll a ball, to plink the toy guitar she gave him. She worked with him steadily the first four years of his life, and then she was transferred to work for the project at another facility. The separation was hard to bear, but for a few years the staff saw to it that Elfreda and Joey were reunited at Christmas. Elfreda was sent in a cab to the holiday party, her lap full of gifts and a big bag of oranges for Joey.

"I wish it could have lasted longer," she says. "If I'd had a car, I could have taken him for rides. I had so much I wanted to teach him."

Before she was admitted to the nursing home, Elfreda went to see Joey one last time. He was nine years old then, and she is certain he recognized her. "He knew me because of the love touch. I did it again that day, and the expression on his face showed me that he remembered."

Joey is fourteen now, in classes, and reports come to

Elfreda that he is not only walking well but is able to run short distances. She smiles shyly. "I hate to say it, but I guess I saved that boy's life. That's bragging, which is terrible, but they say I saved his life, and so I guess I did."

The nursing home is the first home Elfreda has known other than the Fort Wayne houses where she was born and lived for eighty-one years. "How I hated to give up that old house! I kept it up for seventeen years after my husband died. But the neighborhood fell down, and I was robbed, and so I had to move here."

Her two sons visit her often—as do some young men who came into her life after her own sons married and left home. Elfreda likes kids, and her life has been full of them. Walter, for instance, who lived in the neighborhood and came to Elfreda for comfort and reassurance when his parents were quarreling. Walter lives far away now, but he sent her his school graduation picture and a letter that read, "Thank you for teaching me that every person is important."

A former foster grandson phones her twice a month, sends her gifts, and spends several days each summer visiting her "Chuck has a girl now. Maybe they'll get married," says Elfreda Then she laughs and adds, "I'm not jealous. I can't be the only woman in Chuck's life forever."

It is a twist of fate, a seeming injustice, that she was responsible for restoring Joey's spine and is now living only half a life because her own spine is collapsing. But such a thought has never occurred to Elfreda who is a habitually cheerful woman. She does grumble a bit about her confinement but puts it this way, which is typical of Elfreda Brandt: "How in the world can I help anybody from a wheelchair?"

DORA
AND ERNIE

I wouldn't go so far as to promise potential foster grandparents the prospect of a new romance—but it has happened. As I wrote in the foreword, it is not rare for Cupid
to romp through the ranks of the grandparents. One of the
arrows landed in October of 1972—or perhaps it was two
arrows since it was love at first sight for both parties.

It was a big surprise for Dora MacDonald, in whose
mind a second marriage trailed all other thoughts when she
signed up for the Foster Grandparent Program in Wilton,
New York. Dora had divorced her husband a very long
time ago. It hadn't been a happy marriage, possibly because she had married the man out of her loneliness.

Dora was one of those women who devote their lives
to caring for their families. After her parents died when she
was a young girl, she took over as a surrogate mother for
her two brothers and kept house for them. When they left
the nest, Dora found life depressingly empty of purpose.
She was forty-two years old when she married and forty-
six when she sued for divorce.

After that she worked for many years as a secretary in

a New York City hospital and later moved to the Catskill area of New York to keep house for a couple who had twin girls. She frequently took the children down to Manhattan, where she enjoyed buying clothes for them. Long past the age of childbearing, Dora called the twins her babies and wished they were in fact her own. She had tried to adopt a child during her brief marriage but was told she was already too old. Now, though, through the Foster Grandparent Program, she could pretend she had her own, and she looked forward to the orientation process.

She found the class fascinating and perhaps even more so the tidy looking gentleman on the other side of the room. He had a good head of hair for an old man and fine eyes and a nice, strong looking jaw. The staff addressed him as Ernie. Ernie what? Dora wondered and then chided herself for her interest; she should remember she hadn't been married for more than twenty years.

Ernie Anderson noticed Dora immediately; a woman just the right height for him, with pretty hair and lovely eyes and a haunting sort of smile that played about her lips. And he said to himself, no, no, Ernie. He'd been a widower only two years, he was seventy-three years old, and he had no business noticing women.

But there she was, and he couldn't help himself. It was damned lonely living in that house he'd begun building before his wife had died. Even with his son next door and the two grandchildren, nothing filled the empty spaces in his house.

Dora had her camera with her that first day and took a picture of all the new foster grandparents. Then she approached Ernie Anderson.

"Would you take my picture, please?"

"Happy to oblige," said Ernie, who took a snapshot of her that turned out to be headless and has ever after been a joke between them.

As for the picture she took of him, Dora cut it out and

kept it in her locker at the service center where the new grandparents were assigned to work with the children.

Dora began work with Joyce, a twelve-year-old child with Down's syndrome. Despite her handicap, Joyce enjoyed the game Dora brought to the center, and every day was at the top of the stairs to greet her foster grandmother, leading her to the table where Joyce had the game all set up.

Ernie had his boys, Bruce and David, and found a new sense of youth, remembering the days when his own son had been young. He told Dora one day, "I guess I'm like the saying that goes 'twice a boy and once a man.'"

It was a long time before Ernie got around to talking to Dora and she fretted, hoping he would phone her. There was no sense wishing he'd bring her home from the center, because he lived much closer to the building than she did, and, worse luck, in the opposite direction from her apartment.

The first move came after the Christmas party at the center, where the children had decorated a beautiful tree, and the foster grandparents had exchanged small gifts.

"Here, I'll help you get home with those," said Ernie.

She asked him in for coffee, and they sat talking at the kitchen table. Ernie turned out to be a funny fellow, and Dora was a good audience, laughing at and with him in the right places. After that, she asked him to come for dinner. And they began attending church together. Following "work" at the service center they took to wandering along the paths, now covered with snow, and holding hands as they walked.

The program's director noticed, and a small frown creased her brow. The New York State program did not allow married couples to work as foster grandparents—a matter of too much income to qualify—and these two looked serious.

They were, indeed. One night over coffee Ernie swallowed and said, "Dora, I like you."

Her heart thumped.

"Tell you what," he said. "If you were only a little older, maybe ten years, I'd ask you a question."

Now her heart jumped. "I don't know what you're talking about," she said coyly. "But if we're going to discuss age, how old are *you*?"

"Seventy-three."

"Why, Ernie, you're just four years older than I am."

He threw back his head and laughed, and Dora refused to let go of what apparently was her advantage. "What's the question?" she said.

"All right. Will you marry me?"

The news shook up the grandparents at the service center, and the director decided she must speak to the lovebirds. In those days foster grandparents were hard to come by, and the director could ill afford to lose two—particularly a pair doing so well with their assigned children—and she needed to fill her quota for the program.

"I hope you're not jumping into anything," she said. "I know it's none of my business, but . . ."

They only smiled at her. "The wedding's in May," said Dora. "You be there."

The director had to surrender. "They were like two kids who wanted to run off together," she recalls. "Nothing I said made a dent."

Ernie thought of elopement, but that didn't go down well with Dora. They finally agreed the wedding would take place on the mountain—Mt. McGregor where the service center was located—in the building that had formerly served a veterans' organization and had a chapel of its own. David was to stand as Ernie's attendant and Joyce, holding a nosegay, would be Dora's attendant. Both children understood that their "grandparents" were to be married and their own roles at the ceremony, but rehearsal did take a bit longer because of the involvement of the children. Just prior to the wedding day, the other foster grandparents gave Dora and Ernie a surprise party, and then at two o'clock on an afternoon in May of 1973 they were pronounced man and wife.

Nine years later Ernie says, "I asked her in an awful hurry. I didn't know her very well and I jumped at it, but I was lucky. We get along fine." He pauses a moment, his eyes glint with devilment, and he adds, "Considering we haven't got a thing in common."

Dora jumps at the habit. "Why Ernie Anderson, we do too . . ."

"I won't watch your soap operas," he says. "And you don't like country living. Admit it—you're a New Yorker, Dora."

"Not since that last time I went to the city," she says. "Those fresh kids. They pushed past me and then had the nerve to say 'Watch where you're going, you old bag.' And I told them I hoped they'd get sand in their spinach."

Ernie figures it's time to stop teasing and puts an arm around her shoulders. "Stay home with me, honey—that's where it's at."

It's nice to know that the Foster Grandparent Program introduces happiness in so many ways.

FANNY

F anny McNeil had a stroke when she was sixty years old, and although she recovered quite well, she is left with certain limitations. Yoga, for instance, which she used to love, is no longer possible because she cannot perform the physical disciplines. The illness left her feeling useless and with an extraordinary loneliness, a loneliness she's never been able to accept.

A divorcee, Fanny has no children of her own, and the world suddenly seemed a great vacuum. That is why now, three years after her stroke, she insists her work as a foster grandmother stems from a purely selfish motive. "I get so much out of it," she says, "for myself."

Fanny works at San Francisco's General Hospital, where she hovers over children who are ill and comforts their parents. She combs hair, feeds the youngsters, wheels them to X-ray, listens to the problems of teenagers.

There is of course an enormous turnover of patients, with the result Fanny has no sooner gotten to know them than they are discharged, and new little ones fill the empty beds. There are some she remembers vividly, particularly those patients with no knowledge of English, a circumstance quite common in San Francisco's Chinatown, where residents cleave to their mother tongue.

There was the Chinese boy who had been struck by a bus, and surgeons found it necessary to amputate one leg. His bewildered parents had no way of communicating, and when Fanny went to the mother and patted her shoulder, the woman suddenly threw her arms around Fanny in a tight embrace that said more than words ever could.

A freshman in high school, the boy had been an expert tennis player, and now he lay in his bed staring out the window all day long. Fanny sat with him often, gently rubbing his arm, and he sometimes turned to her with his eyes full of tears. Then came the day of celebration when doctors told him a prosthesis would definitely make it possible for him to play tennis again.

Fanny reads to the children and plays games with them in the playroom, where she tries to instill some manners. "You're not the only one here," she says. "You must take only one toy at a time, and take care of it."

She is aghast at the lack of attention received by many children. "They are taught so little at home. Not even how to walk up and down stairs. It seems the parents just grab them and carry them up or down, because it's easier than teaching them how to do it for themselves."

She works with them on that and table manners and how to work with buttons and bows. Most of all, she loves them. The child frightened in the strange milieu, poked and prodded by doctors, terrified of the needles that mean pain, reaches out for Fanny's arms.

She gives happily, a woman who has always so loved children that in her youth she babysat without charging the neighbors in Philadelphia.

Sometimes, Fanny herself needs comforting. It happens when she sees a child suffering an asthma attack or being admitted to pediatrics for what is called FTT—failure-to-thrive.

"It's so awful when the doctors don't know what is

wrong," she says. "That's the scary thing, when all of it really gets to me."

Again, she insists the Foster Grandparent Program seems to be of more benefit to her than to the children. It fills the void of loneliness, and the stipend makes possible her occasional treat of a concert, a ballet, an opera.

Those who know it has been a two-way street, however, are the hundreds of children who have been soothed by Fanny McNeil's loving arms.

OSCAR

I remember meeting Oscar Smith in the spring of 1981—my first Recognition Day for the foster grandparents held at The White House. He is a man with close-cropped, not altogether gray hair and a slight stoop that only hints at his seventy-seven years. He came up to me holding out a large, weather-beaten hand and said, "I've been praying to the Lord, Mrs. Reagan, that you'd shake my hand, so I could tell you that you have the devotion of all the grandparents."

Oscar didn't have to pray. I'd have shaken his hand anyway. But being Oscar, he'd have prayed regardless; he is a dedicated Bible scholar and imparts religious training in dribs, drabs, bits and pieces, whenever he can wedge it between required curriculum at the National Children's Center in Washington, D.C. He has three Bibles and wore one out to the point that he had to have it rebound.

"I am not a man of foolishness," says Oscar. "Since my wife died, I'm fully dedicated to doing something for someone else."

His religious faith is a dividend for the kids at the

center but not the basic reason he is there. Oscar was the very first foster grandparent at the NCC, initially landing among a young staff not at all certain they would want him—or the help being offered by any of these new foster grandparents. After one day with Oscar hugging and roughhousing with the children, the staff decided to contract for nine more. All are women, so that Oscar remains the only grand*father* working at the center. This suits him; it is his distinction. Everyone there—staff, grandmothers, babies just learning to talk—calls him The Grandfather.

Oscar is the antithesis of a chieftain; he is a natural-born teacher, even though he has no formal education beyond high school. On his first day in 1975, the staff gave him a booklet about the center. Reading it at home that night, he noticed a mention about hand language for the deaf, in particular the alphabet imparted by hand gestures. When he evinced interest the following morning, the staff gave him a bigger book, and within seventy-two hours Oscar had mastered the alphabet. Since then he has also become familiar with the actual sign language of the deaf, although he denies he's anywhere near an expert at it.

Watching him work in a classroom refutes his modesty. Leaning over Robbie, who has been "bad" that morning, Oscar grins at him and makes rapid hand movements meaning, "You be good and finish that math problem, and I'll buy you a Coke after lunch."

This delights Robbie who, like all children at the center, so adores Oscar that he vies for his attention. And when Oscar furthers his benevolence by tying Robbie's unruly shoelaces, the boy howls with glee because he has captured grandfather's attention to the exclusion of everyone else.

The alphabet done by hand is invaluable in a facility housing many children who are unable to speak. Because they cannot, whether or not they have hearing impairment, lip reading is invalid. If they do not *know* a word, lip movement means nothing to them. The hands, after all, are the only tools with which we can communicate if voice is not available. And wherever Oscar goes there is a great flurry of hands and fingers, much of it spelling out "Grandfather! Grandfather!"

Oscar's talent stems largely from his Pied Piper charm for the kids, who follow him in both path and pursuit. If he goes into the gym, they are after him, imitating his somersaults, his pushups, the walking on hands. They follow his calisthenics and then line up after him to try the obstacle course, zigzagging their way through a line of tires. When he enters the workshop, they are behind him to learn how to build through numbered and colored blocks. No nails, of course, says Oscar, knowing how suddenly any of the children might become unmanageable.

There is one boy, perhaps special to Oscar although he will not admit to favoritism, who is prone to violence. Gregory was born to a father and mother both of whom are institutionalized as mentally retarded. So there is little hope for this sixteen-year-old, but what can be done is to attempt to make the boy's life more interesting and that of those around him a bit easier. Oscar has taught Gregory how to play basketball. "And he's good at it. He dribbles the ball very well and can shoot hoops. Gregory can be nice, but when he becomes violent, he is a vicious fighter. He lies down and fights with his feet. It's hard to get near him, and the women can't cope. They call me, and I just run in and grab both feet."

Oscar's scope seems unlimited. He is a super baker of cakes, most particularly lemon and chocolate. The staff must supervise the life-skills class, where the kitchen is located, so that Oscar doesn't bake at school. Instead, he fashions his masterpieces, from scratch, at home and then brings them in for everyone to share.

The National Children's Center is what is termed a "fourth resort" facility, meaning that it absorbs children unacceptable to any part of the school system. Therefore, it serves youngsters who are unusually hard to teach. Oscar takes it all with aplomb. He leans over the shoulder of a boy named Steve and on paper spells out the name by outlining it in dots. Steve then connects the dots and thus learns to write his own name. It is a method somewhat like the Montessori system of tracing letters.

"You can't cram anything down a child's throat," says Oscar. "Particularly these children, who will reject pressure. You have to take it slow, take it easy, and have patience." What he doesn't say is that it takes someone who can pretend he still has patience even when he has none left.

Sometimes when The Grandfather is not teaching in class, he can be found sitting in a chair—or on the floor—holding a child in his lap. At first he worked his four hours the usual four days a week but later volunteered an increase to five days. "These children haven't exactly been showered with love, and love is what they need most of all. I teach them and I love them as I would teach and love my own." Oscar motions toward flowers in a vase. "You see those flowers. The children are like them—each beautifies the others. That's the way I feel about these children. My heart goes out to them."

Oscar has children of his own, all grown, sixteen grandchildren "all over the country," plus two great-grandsons. He dotes on his three daughters, remembering with sorrow the son who died in infancy "just when he was starting to walk," and the other son, who died at forty-six "on the bottle." Oscar Smith shakes his head. "He went wrong. He even took the name of the Lord in vain."

Oscar's own father was chauffeur to a state senator in North Carolina, where Oscar was born. He aimed at becoming a chiropractor but failing that worked at loading on docks and "jockeying autos in garages."

After his wife's death, Oscar saved up for a fishing trip in the Bahamas, a lifelong ambition that was not to be. Because one day Oscar Smith, obliging as usual, drove two women who were foster grandparents to visit at a mental hospital and there heard about the FGP. "It was God's plan," says Oscar who shortly thereafter canceled the fishing trip and pinned to his coat lapel the red and gold insignia denoting his foster grandparent involvement.

Occasionally, he takes time off from the children. "I hate to leave the little ones," he says, "but there are elderly people who need my services. I run errands for them, help them pay their little bills." He also visits the sick and on top of that teaches those he calls "oldsters" about Social Security.

Oscar gave up somersaults when he turned sixty-three, and since his seventy-seventh birthday in May, he has been taking things just a touch easier. A heart problem has shown up, necessitating a physical every three months, and as a result he does "only fifteen pushups at a time now."

It's no wonder they all call him grandfather, including Janice, a teacher at the National Children's Center whom Oscar thought was getting kind of fat. Then one day she told him she was pregnant "and not much after that she went off to the hospital and had a pretty little girl. I went over to visit right away, and they wouldn't let me in. They said I had to be a relative. 'Well, I am,' I told them. 'I'm the grandfather.'" Oscar comes close to a giggle telling the story. Imagine a black man telling them at the hospital that he's the grandfather of a white woman. "Or maybe they thought I meant grandfather to the baby," he says. "Anyway, I have a minister's card from a church out in California, so I showed them that, and they finally let me in. I was second to see the baby after the father, and I christened that baby. I have her picture hanging over my bed.

"I sleep well," says Oscar Smith. "I'm ready when the Lord calls me." And when asked what be would choose for an epitaph on his tombstone he said—immediately and with a wide smile—"I'd like it to read 'Here lies grandfather.' That's all."

JEANETTE

To fully understand how Jeanette Gadd could have handled Joey's violence and hatred, it will help to know a little bit about Jeanette. However much you learn, I'm sure you'll enjoy it.

To begin with, she is ninety-one years old. On the day she first applied to become a foster grandparent, she lied about her age, chopping off ten years. You could put it down to vanity if you wanted to, but the truth is that Jeanette looks so much younger than her years that people tend not to believe them and invariably begin the sort of argument Jeanette figures she hasn't time for.

In her initial interview nine years ago down in Fort Lauderdale, Florida, she was eighty-two but stated she was seventy-two.

"You're seventy-two?" repeated the FGP director.

Jeanette bridled slightly "Why? Do I look older than seventy-two?"

"No, no!" the director said. "I'd have said you're in your sixties."

"Thank you," said Jeanette Gadd and grinned to herself, something she does often because she gets a tremendous kick out of life.

Perhaps the reason is that she meets it more than halfway. As a result, stories abound. Take, for example, that very day, the day she applied to the Foster Grandparent Program. Jeanette does not drive and so had asked her daughter, Marie, to take her to the address given her when she had phoned for information. It happened that Marie didn't think her octogenarian mother should get involved yet again in serving others, and at the wheel she kept grumbling about it.

"Really, mom, you're not going to get mixed up with a bunch of kids! Dad has died and you're retired—even though you've already volunteered to help out the March of Dimes—and I don't think you should . . ."

"Just get me there and let me find out what it's all about." Jeanette stared straight ahead. "I haven't said I'd take the job!"

An hour later daughter Marie was still circling in Fort Lauderdale, unable to find the address, and Jeanette was looking grimmer by the minute. "You're just saying you can't find the place because you don't want to take me there!"

"Now, mom," remonstrated Marie.

In a neighborhood totally foreign to both, they passed a tumbledown house on a corner, and Jeanette told her daughter to stop the car. "I'm going in there and ask them if they can tell me where this darned address is."

Marie sighed, stopped the car, turned off the ignition.

"The place looks terrible," said Jeanette. "If I'm not out of there in five minutes, call the cops."

She walked to the shanty's front door and knocked. A girl peered through the opened crack. "What you want?"

As Jeanette began to reply, the door was slammed in her face. A Cadillac pulled to a stop behind Marie's car, and an immense black woman emerged from it and waddled to where Jeanette stood.

"What do you want?" Her tone was threatening.

"Could you help me, please? I'd like to find out where this address is," said Jeanette, showing a slip of paper.

The woman pounded on the door and yelled, "Let us in!"

Jeanette had never seen such a place. The front room was unusual because of the row of telephones, and in contrast to the outside of the house, the interior looked like a movie set. White satin drapes were at the windows, and the furniture was covered with satin, too.

Drugs, thought Jeanette, I'll bet these people are dealing in drugs.

Ordered by the large woman to follow her, Jeanette passed through a dining room she mentally labeled gorgeous, then down a hall past bedrooms done in white satin with canopies over the beds. She followed the woman into a posh office where the madam (and that's a literal term) asked once again what Jeanette was looking for. After being given explicit directions to reach the address written on her slip of paper, Jeanette thanked the woman and went back to her daughter.

"Such a place," she told Marie. "Gorgeous. You should see the furniture and the bedrooms!"

"Holy Toledo!" said Marie, and filled her mother in on the nature of the business.

"I wish I'd seen the upstairs," said Jeanette, then added, "I wonder how much madams make. Maybe I should have stayed there."

"*Mom!*" said Marie.

Well, that's one story about Jeanette. Only the first one.

It was almost a year before she joined the FGP, a busy year that followed Jeanette's tossing the application into a drawer and forgetting about it before going up to New York to visit friends for the summer. Then Marie had spinal surgery, and Jeanette went back to Florida to help out during her daughter's recuperation period. While cleaning drawers, she came across the neglected application. She would have to fill it out right away, she thought. It wasn't good to apply for a job and then not follow up on it, because you never knew when you might need a reference from the people involved.

How did a woman in her eighties come to have thoughts worthy of a business executive? Because Jeanette Gadd had grown up in Brooklyn and had gone through the New York public-school system before she attended Brown's Business College. She not only graduated from Brown's but went on to take assorted classes at Columbia University—in the days at the turn of the century when women were looked down upon for "going to business," and few finished high school, let alone attending college. She was a secretary for a department of welfare, then worked for the War Department, and followed that with a twenty-year stint at the Industrial Home for the Blind, where she managed a professional library. It was a background to impart moxie to a woman living in that period.

Jeanette retired only because of her husband's failing health. She had been temporarily stunned by the sudden death of their son who left a widow and two small children, but Jeanette only skidded a bit and was soon back on her track.

The widowed daughter-in-law asked Jeanette if she would mind if she moved to Florida. "I ask because I've always said I'd never take the kids away from you."

"If *we* moved to Florida, which I doubt," said Jeanette, "we wouldn't ask you for permission. Go on, do what you want."

With that part of the family removed, it wasn't long before her husband wanted to move to Florida too. Jeanette acquiesced, and hated it. A native New Yorker, she complained, "I can't stand this place! They pull in the sidewalks at nine o'clock!"

There followed a push-and-pull period of well over a

year during which Jeanette kept visiting New York and loving every minute of it and then going back to her husband in Florida, because that's where he wanted to be. She finally forfeited the concerts, the delicatessens, the night life, the bustle of New York, and settled down permanently in Florida—and was grateful she had surrendered when her husband died not long after.

Which brings us back to the point where Jeanette had discovered the forgotten FGP application and had sat down to fill it out. The phone rang at that moment, and on the other end of the line was the FGP supervisor.

"I was just writing you," said Jeanette. "I'm so sorry I forgot to send you the application, and I'll send a letter of apology with it."

"Forget the letter," said the supervisor. "I have a place for you, working in the public schools with special children."

"I can't take the job," said Jeanette. "I don't drive, and my daughter is too ill to drive me."

"We have a woman who will pick you up every morning. I'll come to your place now, and you can give me the application. Will you start tomorrow?"

And that's how Jeanette began in the Foster Grandparent Program.

She was asked to work with the first grade. And in first grade was Joey, who had been the terror of the school during two previous years in kindergarten. Joey's home life was a horror. His alcoholic father brutally attacked his mother almost daily, and Joey watched the struggle as his mother screamed and tried to escape the man's blows. It was all Joey knew, had ever known, and in school he bit and kicked the other children. His attitude was sullen; he seemed to want an argument, any excuse to inflict injury on others.

Joey was beginning his third year of disruptive behavior when he and Jeanette landed in the same classroom.

Of course she realized immediately how troubled the boy was, and she frequently watched after he'd done something such as wallop another child with a chair and was carried bodily from the room by a counselor, squirming in resistance with all the force he could muster.

She often saw him watching her. A sidelong glance would reveal Joey staring at her, and the fact gave Jeanette hope that she might have some influence on him. Her attempts so far had failed miserably. She had tried being nice, and that hadn't worked. She had announced that she was in command, and that *certainly* hadn't worked. So she ignored him for a while, and that's when she noticed, while working with other children, that Joey never took his eyes off her.

One day she purposely left a book on the table next to Joey's, its pages opened to the story of Jack the Giant Killer. Later, as she passed it and him she said, "What is this, a storybook? Did you see this, Joey?"

He shook his head.

"Gee," she said. "I haven't read that since I was a little girl. Would you like me to read this with you?"

He didn't reply, and Jeanette took the book to his table and spread it open between them. While he sat and listened, he kept moving away from her, little by little, and when the morning break was over Jeanette said, "I guess we'll have to continue this tomorrow. Did you enjoy it?"

For a moment he said nothing, then, "Can I keep the book?"

"It belongs to the school, but if you take very good care of it you may keep it in your desk. And we'll read it again tomorrow."

The next day she was working with another child when Joey approached, hands jammed into his pockets. "You gonna read to me today?"

"Later," she said.

Two more mornings and they had finished the story.

191

Then she said, "We haven't looked at your regular reader, Joey. Suppose we try that."

Then began a display of body language, with the woman inching toward him, and the boy pulling away from her. He seemed fascinated, though, by the reading process, and one day when he was particularly engrossed Jeanette said, "This book isn't big enough to stretch out so we can see it together. I'm just going to have to move closer to you."

That day he allowed it, and within a week was even permitting other children to stop and speak to Jeanette. Previously he had yelled and threatened to hit them if they so much as hesitated in walking by his table.

"You like baseball cards?" she asked him, and when he nodded, she said, "I have a bunch. Every day you read well for me I'm going to give you one."

By the time they finished the reader, Joey was almost sitting on top of her. By now she could even put her arm around him, and he wouldn't move away.

"You're a smart boy," she told him. "Just as good as the other kids, and from now on you can get in line with your class and read with them. And Joey, don't argue with them. They like you, and they want to be friends with you, so you be friends with them, okay?"

The first day after Jeanette and Joey had finished their work together, and he was to join the regular class, he silently came up to her and put his arms around her.

Jeanette isn't given to tears the way I am, but that day she wept inside for joy.

With her late son's two children and daughter Marie's son, Jeanette is by now the grandmother of three and the great-grandmother of two. Marie tells her she suspects Jeanette thinks more of the kids at school than she does of her own young family.

"Don't be ridiculous," says Jeanette. "My own gang is around every day, and these little children aren't. I listen to

192

all their little tales and woes. Our own kids are well taken care of, they don't have any woes."

She can go on forever about the schoolchildren. There was Wendy, the timid little girl Jeanette noticed always standing alone between classes. One day Jeanette saw that she was crying and asked what was the matter. When the child didn't respond Jeanette said, "Will you do me a favor? I'm eating lunch with my class, but I like to have a special guest. Would you be my guest today and eat with us?" The girl took Jeanette's hand on the way into the cafeteria where Jeanette told her class, "This little girl stands outside with no one to eat with. She's my guest today, and I want you to make her feel at home with us."

This went on for three mornings, and then Jeanette asked Wendy where her own class was and took her there, giving her classmates the same speech. "She has been my guest every day this week, so today I'd like to be your guest. When I leave, you girls will take care of your friend, won't you?" The next day Jeanette saw Wendy with her own classmates clustered around her, laughing and talking. And later, as Jeanette sat talking with a teacher, Wendy sneaked up behind her and kissed the back of her neck. When Jeanette looked around, Wendy said, "I love you."

There was Melinda, the black girl with the imagination that worked overtime. Melinda was an able student and therefore not slated for the help of a foster grandparent, but she apparently resented this, asking Jeanette why she didn't work with her.

"Because I don't select the kids I work with. Ask your teacher. She's the one who tells the grandmas which children to work with. But I don't think you need help, dear."

The following day Jeanette was ganged up on by five small black boys demanding to know why she didn't work with Melinda. Jeanette went to the teacher (which Melinda hadn't bothered to do) and said, "I think we're in trouble. They think this is racial discrimination, and Melinda's boyfriends weren't very nice about it this morning." The teacher agreed that to avoid friction Jeanette should work on a page or two with Melinda each day, which should satisfy the child and her friends.

Jeanette promised Melinda she would work with her the next morning. But when morning came there was an emergency needing Jeanette's attention, and she had to cancel her brief session with Melinda. "I'll work with you tomorrow," she said.

Melinda's jaw came forward. "I can't come tomorrow 'cause my mom is having a baby, and I'm taking her to the hospital."

When Melinda showed up in class the next day, Jeanette asked why she wasn't at the hospital.

"Well, when I explained to my mom about you working with me, she said she'd wait 'til Saturday to have the baby, so here I am."

The lie was so ingenious that Jeanette shouldn't have been at all surprised when Melinda later told her that her real grandmother had died the preceding night. Jeanette was shocked; by this time she knew Melinda well enough to be aware that the grandmother took care of five children while the mother worked. "What happened?" she wanted to know.

"She choked to death," said Melinda.

Jeanette bit, hook, line, and sinker. "Good heavens. How?"

"Well, you know what God does to people that steal."

"*Steal?*"

"Yeah. She got up during the night and was stealing my candy, so she choked to death."

Regarding the racial issue at school, Jeanette has just about settled it, all by herself. It began with her pity for a small black boy who kept failing in games with other boys. Then on a morning after the kids had had a tug of war on field day, Jeanette came to school and was confronted by the boy holding a pennant and grinning from ear to ear. "Look, grandma! I won!"

She grabbed him and kissed him, whereupon a boy named Mike, who followed Jeanette like a shadow, objected. "Hey grandma, no fair. You kissed him."

"And why shouldn't I? He deserves a lot of credit."

"Because he's black," said Mike.

"He's not black inside," Jeanette said. "It's only his skin that's black, the same as yours is white and some are yellow."

"Why are people yellow?" Mike wanted to know, and Jeanette's imagination took off, far exceeding anything Melinda could have whipped up.

"Well, I'll tell you. When God was mixing the dye, he didn't have enough left, and what he did have left he put some of this on one and some of that on the other."

Hearing of this splendid explanation, daughter Marie shook her head. "I don't know how you think up that stuff!"

"Easy," said Jeanette.

The children have given her both pleasure and laughter—the small boy who waited on her hand and foot, wouldn't even let her carry her own pocketbook between class and cafeteria. "That's too heavy for you, grandma. I'll carry it."

And the boy who asked if she used hairspray.

"Of course I do," said Jeanette. "I wallow in it. Why do you ask?"

"'Cause you smell just like my mom."

"Does she smell nice?"

"Oh, yes. She smells beautiful, and she is beautiful. Just like you."

Not all were so complimentary. Freddie was stumped when the teacher asked the class to write what they'd like to be when they grew up. Jeanette was there to help the children with spelling, and Freddie tugged at her jacket, saying he didn't know what he wanted to be.

"What does your dad do?"

"He's a bone doctor."

"Then you be a bone doctor. Tell you what, Freddie. you be a bone doctor, and I'll wait for you, and then I'll be your girlfriend."

Freddie looked at her and scowled. "You'll be *much* too old for me," he said.

That innocent insult was delivered by a boy who had reported to his parents his affection for Jeanette ("Nobody does anything right around there except grandma") with whom he was now the best of friends, and yet their initial meeting had been a clash of wills. When Jeanette first began working with Freddie's class, he told her he wanted a pencil.

"Come here," she said. "You don't get anyting from me unless you say please may I have it. And after you get it you will say thank you."

"Those are three words I don't like," announced Freddie.

"Really? Well, I like them, and if you don't use them with me, you and I are not going to get along at all."

He turned on his heel and walked away. About ten yards. Then he turned and came back to stand in front of her. "Well—if that's the way you want it . . . ."

In contrast, Amy gave Jeanette the ultimate compliment. Having proclaimed she would be a teacher when she grew up, Amy went on to say that she would be a nice teacher and a kind teacher and all the kids would love her.

"I'm sure they will," smiled Jeanette.

"I have one problem. I need a favor from you," said Amy.

"And what is that?"

"You've got to be the classroom grandma."

Jeanette did some silent arithmetic; she'd be at least 113 years old. "I'd consider that an honor," she said.

One doesn't forget Jeanette Gadd in a hurry, if ever. I remember meeting her in 1976 when I visited the program in Fort Lauderdale. She greeted me at the door and handed me a corsage. That in itself wasn't so memorable, but then she introduced me to the small boy at her side. "Travis, I want you to meet our next First Lady," she said. This meant nothing to the child, of course, and she followed it with, "First Lady means this is the wife of our next president."

And then at the end of the tour, there was Jeanette bending over a desk with Travis, who was tracing words in his reader with one finger. I went to sit by them, and she asked if I'd like to hear Travis read, and of course I said yes. He struggled through three pages, and Jeanette said, "Wasn't that wonderful, Mrs. Reagan?" But Travis wasn't about to be dismissed; he announced he would read the entire book to me.

"No you're not," said Jeanette. "I've pressed my luck far enough with three pages."

My staff was signaling to me that I was running late on my schedule, and it was time to leave. But I was so enchanted with this pair that I said, "No, no. I want to hear Travis read some more. I'll let you know when I'm ready to go."

I later learned that Jeanette's pocketbook had been grabbed by a mugger (apparently on a day when it wasn't being toted by her small slave). She had distinguished herself that day by chasing the man for six blocks. Two teachers and a man in a car took up the chase, but for a while Jeanette was in the lead—until a cooler head prevailed. A woman appeared on the scene and stopped Jeanette cold. "I don't care what's in your bag," she told the octogenarian. "You are not going to run another step or you'll drop dead."

"I almost had him!" crowed Jeanette. "His hair was blowing backward, and I almost got a fistful of it!"

Atypically, Jeanette will admit—rarely—that sometimes she's tired when she gets out of bed in the morning. "I think I won't go into work that day, and then I talk to myself and say, 'what's the use of sitting around home all day?'"

At a time she had a serious bout with the flu, she told her daughter, "I can't die, I won't die. If I die I'll miss those kids, and I couldn't stand that."

At last report, she had claimed the honor of being the oldest foster grandparent in the Fort Lauderdale program. Her true age had been kept secret for years, even after Jeanette had confessed to the program director. On a day when all were attending a workshop meeting, a foster grandmother objected to the claim of another that she was the eldest. "She's not," said the woman. "I am. I'm eighty."

With ninety-one years behind her, Jeanette squirmed, barely able to keep quiet, and then the program director caught her eye.

"May I tell them, Jeanette? It's time we all knew the truth."

"Go ahead," said Jeanette. "What do I care? I'm not looking for an old man. I'm very satisfied with my life."

She certainly is.

ARTHUR

W hen you first look into Arthur Gordon's eyes you
know he's going to say something interesting. Or
funny. There's a twinkle that can't be missed, and the message is a valid one, for Arthur is a man of fine intelligence.

He has been a professional writer and an equally professional dog breeder, having bred and trained beagles that
won Best of Show in such elite dog shows as Madison
Square Garden's. Of his experience with dogs, Arthur
admits to an appalling ignorance at the start. "My wife
wanted a hunting dog, and so once we'd moved to
California from New York we looked at ads in the local paper, and alphabetically, beagles came first. We bought a
pair, and then one day I went to a dog show and looked at
the beagles there. I went home and looked again at ours
and decided either ours or theirs were not beagles, and so
we began collecting real beagles."

Of his writing career he says, "I've done art reviews
and reviewed jazz records. I've sort of run the gamut on the
typewriter—I once even edited a book about aviation for a
Bulgarian barnstorm flyer. He was a lousy writer, but he

had the information. The trouble was that he thought in Bulgarian. I had to translate all that Bulgarian thought into English, but I guess that's my forte—I can transform complex things into something simple."

He most certainly can. Arthur should have been a teacher.

His talent has served him well in his present occupation as a foster grandfather in Santa Cruz County, about seventy miles south of San Francisco. Arthur has worked with mentally retarded children for the past eight years, and no one is more surprised than he at his success. He is seventy-seven years old, has lived alone for fourteen years since his divorce, and according to stereotype, this would limn him as a crotchety old character, uninterested in anything other than his own comfort—and complaining about the lack of it. Arthur does not fit the picture. In point of fact, he dislikes most people in his age bracket.

"Can't stand 'em," he says. "There's a generation gap between us. They sit around playing bingo and griping about the world in a mindless way. And if you're different from them in any way—dress, haircut, conversation— they'll crucify you. I'll give you an example. In the checkout line at the market yesterday a voice behind me said, 'You know, the more you pay these checkers, the slower they get.' Now the girl was doing her job at a decent pace, and I turned around to see who'd made the crack. It was an old guy, of course. So I asked him if he could save five minutes, what was he going to do with them when he got home? Play checkers? He looked at me as though I'd betrayed our whole generation."

Unlike those he describes, Arthur does not belabor the subject but instead gets on with constructive conversation relating to the children who enhance what he is loathe to admit *is* his old age. He has a remarkable understanding of his charges and, I think, can impart this understanding to the rest of us better than most grandparents, so much so that I've decided to let Arthur speak for himself in my book. After all, he's a professional writer, and that talent combined with his innate teaching ability is good reason to let Arthur Gordon take over here.

"My childhood was so far behind me that when I first thought about joining the Foster Grandparent Program I had to question how I'd be able to reach these kids. But I discovered there was no problem. These children are so emotionally deprived that they reach out for you. All you have to do is return the feeling, and you're an instant success.

"Maybe I knew what to do with kids—even though I never had any of my own—because I'd gone through a good deal of psychotherapy and afterward had edited a lot of books on the subject. By the time I'd spent a couple of years on the couch mumbling about my dreams, every analyst in New York was writing a book. So I learned a lot about *why* kids are mentally ill, the things people do to them, and after that I always thought that if I every did have any children I'd be a pretty good dad.

"The first thing I had to learn was patience. The youngsters learned so slowly, and finally I realized it was my fault because I'd been pushing them at my own pace. That was wrong, and I forced myself to slow down.

"There's a lot to learn about the mentally retarded. One thing is that they think more than you would surmise. They've been told all their lives, for instance, that they're stupid, that they can't do anything right. It's not long before they're ashamed of themselves. And they have pride. Ergo, they're not about to admit they don't understand anything. It follows that they don't have the sort of dedication we have for self-improvement. They simply try to hide their inadequacy. One result of this is that they refuse to practice. It would be impossible to teach tennis to a mentally retarded kid because to learn the game he must practice—and if he practices, that in itself means he doesn't yet know how. You can imagine, therefore, how difficult it is to teach them any new skill.

"An example of hiding inadequacy is a middle-aged man I know who was pretty good at computation unless he was required to do it in a hurry. So when he went to the market, he would stuff his pockets with five- and ten-dollar bills. If the checker told him the bill was three dollars and thirty-eight cents, he'd whip out a five, knowing he was safe, thinking this would hide the fact there was something he didn't do well.

"When the kids are learning to read and come to a word they don't understand, they will slur over it rather than admit they don't know it by asking. I never let a child get by with that. I stop his reading and say, 'What was that word again?' Of course he can't answer, and so I ask him if he wants to be smart or stupid. When he answers smart, I tell him the difference. 'When you don't know a word and try to make believe you do, that is dumb. Smart is when you don't know, but you ask.' They don't understand this right away, but when you start praising them for having asked, they'll often begin the habit of asking.

"Along these same lines, while they are ashamed of not knowing, they are enormously proud of knowing. That's the reason our kids love repetitive jobs and skills. Most people would go nuts doing the same thing over and over, but to these kids it means that after being reminded all their lives they are worthless, they have suddenly learned to do something worthwhile. They love the mastery of a skill—and it does not require memory.

"We have to remember that the one thing these children have in common is a rotten memory. If they could remember what they learn, then they wouldn't be backward. For instance, you tell them two and three make five, and three seconds later they'll ask you how much are two and three. But there's a way. I learned it when we took the kids on a trip through a commercial bakery. First, the kids were given a lecture about using whole wheat flour instead of white and that they used honey instead of sugar. Each kid was given a little lump of dough, which they were allowed to toss into the oven, and then we went through the place. When we came back in a half hour, their loaves were finished, and while they sat around munching the warm bread, the man in charge said, 'Now what kind of flour do we use?'

"I braced myself for the silence that was sure to follow, and then, to my amazement, they all yelled 'Whole wheat!' And when he asked what was used for sweetening, they were right on target with 'Honey!'

"And so I learned something. Three plus two is an abstraction, and they just don't get it. But bread that's tasty and warm that you've made yourself, that's interesting; and they'll remember everything about it. Now I realize I must try to equate that they are learning with an experience that's pleasurable to them. They teach me how to teach.

"Prior to the Foster Grandparent Program I'd never taught anything to anyone, but I think I know what helps me. As a writer, I had to learn how to communicate, and when I was given an assignment, my first question to myself was, who was going to read it. Then I directed the writing to the particular interest, the particular mentality. When I teach, it works the same way, so I've known how to talk to these kids. I've heard certified teachers tell the mentally retarded child, 'Listen, son, you've got to learn how to behave like an adult.' The boy being spoken to doesn't even understand the meaning of the word *adult*.

"You have to take it slowly. For example, Ruthie was one of my brighter girls in the program, but I had difficulty in teaching her the difference between odd and even numbers. I spent weeks at it before I finally got the answer. I asked her how many shoes she'd get if she bought a pair, and she said two. Then I said, 'If the salesman gave you only one shoe, would you take it?' Of course she said no, and after I gave her a quiz on how many shoes in two pair, three pair, et cetera, she finally understood odd and even.

"Tim was better in math than most, and once he'd mastered a level, I'd raise him to the next. Typical of wanting to perform well, he complained he never had time to 'play' with what he'd just learned before I put him on to something new that he couldn't answer. So the next day I gave him a whole bunch of easy stuff he'd already learned and then asked him if he'd enjoyed the lesson. He said no, and I explained it was because it had been too easy, that he hadn't learned anything. Smart, I told him, is when you learn something more, and he shouldn't be afraid of making mistakes, because it isn't a mistake the first time but only the second time.

"The small goal with the retarded is to make their lives even a little bit happier. But there is the larger goal of making them self-reliant to the point they can be independent. Achieved, this goal means they can move out of the foster home or the group home and live by themselves. Some even get jobs and marry. In the past the teaching has taken place within special schools, but the new focus is to get the kids out into the world. It's called 'mainstreaming,' and it involves getting the kids out to mix with the public. This not only prepares them for life outside the institution, it helps get the public accustomed to seeing them.

"Almost all retarded kids have a distorted facial expression; it's bad enough for a person to move to a new city and be regarded suspiciously because he's a stranger, but add to that the fact he *looks* different, and he's in real trouble. Thus, there is mainstreaming to make them comfortable and, hopefully, to make them accepted. We take the kids on field trips on the bus, to restaurants, to the zoo, to stores, any place where they can walk around in groups and see and be seen. While they are learning to be comfortable, the public is learning to accept the presence of the retarded, including those afflicted with Down's syndrome, which has commonly been described as mongolism.

"In mainstreaming I've worked with a great teacher named Shirley Smith. I say she's great because instead of insisting on curriculum, she has encouraged me to try new things, to work more individually with each child. Since we were selected to work as a team on mainstreaming, we've worked on teaching the kids how to make decisions, a thing they've never been called upon to do. Riding on a public bus for the first time they must select the right bus, pay the right fare, get off at the right stop. They must learn how to tell time so that they know what time to take the bus back home.

"This is particularly important when they begin work after turning twenty-one at what are called 'skill centers.' Here they do simple jobs: packaging things, making candles, and some are even sent out on custodial crews where they clean stores and offices at night. These jobs are available, of course, only to the more capable. For the others I've done things as simple as having them vote each day for a different child to do the job of calling the roll. It's not simple for them—they must make a decision.

"When we take them to stores they must decide what department they want to look at and, if they have money of their own, what to buy. All this is a big step for them.

"We've instituted a program wherein several of our kids attend a regular school. During the first year a large number of Chicano children had been enrolled, and I was wary about this because it's been my experience that every minority group looks for a minority group they consider lower than themselves on the scale and proceeds to persecute them. I could have saved myself the worry, because something wonderful happened there. When I first saw the Chicano kids I thought, my God, they're going to kill our poor kids, but, instead, they became marvelous friends. I can't figure this unless it's because they didn't feel rejected or threatened by our kids and so treated them like little brothers and sisters.

"At the school we put our kids to work learning vocational habits. Many of the girls worked at cleaning up in the cafeteria, and every day we'd put one in the serving line where, like all the regular employees, she'd put food on the students' trays. This helped get our youngsters accepted, because they did the same things as normal people. The acceptance has been so great, incidentally, that the normal kids at the school have begun to volunteer their help in such droves that we've had to turn some of them down.

"We have a training farm, too, set up by an instructor named Dick Struck who felt our kids could learn simple tasks in animal husbandry. They love working at the farm where they collect eggs, clean the stables and pens, as well as planting and caring for crops. They learn how to raise cactus in the greenhouse there, and they grow vegetables. The pumpkins are so great that they are collected every October by service organizations in the area. As for animal husbandry, many have joined the Future Farmers of America, and some have even won prizes for their livestock at local fairs.

"I repeat my belief that the mentally retarded experience more thought and emotion than many people think they do, and I have a favorite story I think proves the point. You've probably heard of the Special Olympics, by now an international program of sports training and athletic competition for mentally retarded children and adults. I was working in the Foster Grandparent Program when the Special Olympics began, at first with only four events. The kids had to throw a baseball, run fifty yards, do a standing broad jump, and jump over a bar. We had two boys here, good friends who were fine athletes. In the various fifty-yard sprints, they won on the local level within their own divisions and finally competed against the others. Both went on to the regional olympics held at UCLA, and the same thing happened: each won in various heats and then competed along with others in the final event. When the one leading the race looked over his shoulder and saw that his friend was just behind him, he slackened pace so his pal could catch up with him, and they crossed the finish line together. The audience cheered wildly, and I saw several people weeping.

"I want to make the point here that while I may have had some success with our kids, they have done an awful lot for me. I'm not only healthy, which I think is due in part to my involvement with the Foster Grandparent Program, but I think I've discovered the secret of old age. I've heard so many people say that when they retire they're going to play golf every day once they've taken trips to the places they've yearned to see all their lives. Well, they retire and they go to all those places and discover, whether or not they admit it, that the places they wanted to see when they were twenty-five are not as exciting as they thought they'd be when they're seventy-five.

"I think I've learned a bit in my seventy-seven years, and I'm grateful to the FGP for allowing me to make use of it. This program is something for the heart. Because the one paramount need in old age is that of being needed."

As for me, I'm grateful to Arthur Gordon. Better than anyone I know he tells what it is like to be a foster grandparent and what it accomplishes for the children.

I'm told he was asked by the teacher at the training farm what he would like the children to call him. Arthur said it didn't matter to him, and the teacher suggested the use of "Mr. Gordon." "Because I want the children to respect you," he added.

"I don't want them to respect me," said Arthur. "I want them to like me."

He has his wish. It's been reported to me that every day he arrives at the training farm, a throng of kids runs to him, vying with each other to be he first to throw arms around grandpa Arthur.

MARGE

In Grand Rapids, Michigan, there is a center provided for women who are abused by men. It takes in the victims and their children, who live there for as long as necessary until a resolution has been reached. They are provided with beds, and the women cook together in a communal kitchen. Their children are with them except for the hours when the women are in counseling or training sessions with the staff professionals.

At those times, someone must care for the children, and that's the service Marge Hager offered for about one month during her five-year stint for the FGP—which otherwise has been devoted to working within the public-school system.

Of the center she says, "People don't come to that place unless it is out of desperation, and so the children coming there live in a desperate situation." The first day she worked there the woman in charge of the children had just quit, and the director of the FGP had left on vacation. There were fourteen children, including a few babies, so Marge rolled up her sleeves and went to work. It was easier when the staff was complete, but then came Ralph, and Ralph was the toughest nut of all to crack.

She remembers him as a five-year-old boy who came to the center with his brother, sister, and mother. His siblings behaved reasonably well, but at five, Ralph was at an age when a rift between parents hits the hardest. When the time came to take him from his mother, he clung to her and had to be pried away and propelled downstairs to the playroom or outdoors to the play yard. Every day, he beat on the door through which he had seen his mother leave. Marge tried to calm him, putting him in her lap and holding his thrashing arms and legs. He struggled to get away from her, pounding her with his small fists. "I hate you! I hate you!" he screamed.

Each time he said it, Marge replied in a calm voice, "But I love you."

One day, she recalled, he stood at the top of a flight of stairs where he had been beating in vain on a closed door. Marge was on a lower floor, and when he caught sight of her he said, "Grandma?" "Yes," she said, and he put one foot on a lower step and called her a filthy name. And then, one step at a time, he called to her, and when she answered, he hurled abusive language at her. They were words Ralph knew well in his home environment, even though he was too young to know their meaning. The vulgarisms continued, one for each of the eighteen steps, and Marge only looked up at him and smiled.

It happened that the day Ralph and his family were to leave the center was also Marge's day of departure; her doctor had detected a heart problem that would no longer allow her to work in the building because of the stairs. Neither the boy nor the elderly woman had any way of knowing they would never see each other again when they met by chance in the kitchen.

"Where you goin'?" he asked her.

"I'm going home," she said. "I won't be coming here any more."

Ralph ran to her and put his arms around her legs. "I love you, Grandma," he said.

Marge wept a bit at that, and ever since, although she has allowed herself to suspect the boy had softened only because he knew he was going home at last, that maybe, just maybe, he really *did* feel that he loved her.

RUTH

Of them all, she is perhaps the bravest. I use the word "perhaps" because I don't know if the others may have secrets they haven't opened to the light, thus inviting censure and even scorn.

Ruth has summoned the courage to tell her story truly and candidly, and because of this, risks the shock waves that will surely run through the ranks of her friends in Denver, most particularly the other foster grandparents who, when they read this, will know of Ruth's past for the first time.

When she was approached regarding inclusion in my book, she was told that each chapter would consist of the story of a foster grandparent, as well as that person's work with a child or children. Ruth agonized over her decision. If she told the truth about the months in a mental institution, the years lived in prison, would her friends turn away from her? More importantly, would her disclosure of her long record as a felon preclude inclusion in a book designed to describe "nice" people?

Her final decision turned entirely on Tiffany, her foster

grandchild. If the plight of Tiffany were told, maybe someone, somewhere, would take an interest and offer help.

Ruth cooperated to the fullest, but with one request—
that her last name not be used. Her son and daughter, she
said, had suffered enough because of her decadence; she
would not further embarrass them today by associating
them with her. So we will not tell you Ruth's full identity.
But they will know in Denver. And because she is a
woman of fortitude, Ruth takes that chance, along with a
prayer that she will be forgiven.

My personal reaction has been sheer delight in discovering a woman of such strength, sensitivity, and intelligence who combines the very best of my two deepest in-
terests, the Foster Grandparent Program and the fight
against drugs—and who represents victory in both.

Her own story comes first and afterward, the achievement with Tiffany, "the surprise of the institution" at
Colorado's Ridge State Home for the profoundly retarded.

Ruth had married, had her two children, and divorced
her husband before she began using heroin. Today, as she
searches her inner self for a reason for starting the habit,
she realizes that the postdivorce period, when she was
alone in the struggle to support her family, was only the
surface rationale. Deeper was her innate need for a surfeit
of love; she felt she had never been given enough. Her
father had been a cold and distant man, and while her
mother performed every maternal duty, she was not a de-
monstrative woman. Ruth had sorely missed outward pro-
fessions of love in both her childhood and marriage. (It is
one reason why, as a foster grandparent, she knows so well
the importance of that kind of love.)

Whatever the provocation, she was well acquainted
with the use of drugs because several friends were addicts,
and she knew where and how to get heroin. Temple Street
in Los Angeles was the place to "score," and if you were
smart, you did it in the daytime. The cops were much more

prevalent in that area at night. She considered herself too street smart to be caught and had been using heroin for five years before her first arrest.

It happened when she disregarded her self-imposed rule to stay off the streets at night. Totally addicted by now, she badly needed to score and with two girlfriends went to a cafeteria at Second and Hill Streets at nine o'clock at night to pick up the dope. She carried all of it, hers and theirs, in two balloons tucked into her mouth as they started the four-block walk back to Ruth's apartment. As they were walking through the tunnel that connects two main streets, they were stopped by narcotics officers. One man grabbed Ruth around the throat, and she tried to swallow the balloons as he thrust a hand into her mouth. She bit his fingers savagely—addicts will fight like wild things to get and keep their drugs—but he was too quick for her. The evidence for possession was there.

First possession had always meant a mandatory sentence of from six months to six years, and Ruth knew it. Nevertheless she refused to squeal on her two friends, and the police never learned that part of the dope had been bought by the other girls. All three were taken to the Hill Street station, but Ruth was the only one arrested.

She spent six months in the county jail awaiting sentence. They took her repeatedly to court, where she continued to refuse a probation hearing. That would have meant putting her family through an investigation for probation, and Ruth felt certain she wouldn't get probation anyway. They would sentence her to prison regardless, so why bother with all the fancy details.

It evolved that, although she knew as much as any addict, all of whom absorb a knowledge of the law because they must know enough to dodge it, there was something she did not know. A new law had just gone into effect: first possession now carried a sentence of from one to twenty years. Ruth was given thirty months "behind the gate" with a ten-year parole to follow, and she did her time in the California Institute for Women.

The institute was a comparatively humane, modern prison, with its inmates on the honor system. But Ruth was a rebel by nature. She chafed under her sentence, figuring she had harmed no one other than herself and that she did not deserve punishment. Sure, the C.I.W. was fairly decent for a jail, but it didn't matter where you were locked up—the fact remained you'd lost your freedom. She describes herself as "a bad actor" during those three years of incarceration. She'd show them; she took delight in breaking rules in a way that precluded censure. As an example, inmates were required to wear a belt. Ruth wore a heavy chain around her neck, and when she was called to task and asked where her belt was, she smiled benignly and said, "Here. I'm wearing it around my neck."

She didn't always escape punishment. She had been in "the hole" (solitary) for several days when her mother made the regular Sunday visit and was shocked because Ruth was not tidy, in fact not even clean. Her mother was so incensed that she burst into the warden's office insisting on better treatment. She even phoned Governor Brown, pleading with him for leniency for the daughter "locked up with all those criminals." As long as she lived, Ruth's mother was unrelenting in her support and aghast that her daughter was actually in jail.

"My mother was so naïve about the law," Ruth recalls, "that she truly thought I'd be sent to a hospital instead of jail."

When she came out of prison, Ruth found a job running an employment agency in the San Fernando Valley, where it was said she did the best job of anyone they'd ever hired. She was free from her heroin habit, she had a salary, an apartment, and her children with her again. For three years they had been in a Baptist children's home and later assigned to a foster home.

All might have gone well for her had she not fallen in

love with a man we'll call John. Shakespeare wrote that we can be defiled by the company we keep, and so it was with Ruth, whose acquaintances as an addict had been almost entirely limited to other addicts. John was not an addict but something worse: he was a drug dealer. He traveled a lot, and Ruth knew what he was doing—either going somewhere to buy the stuff or somewhere else to sell it. His source of income was tacitly acknowledged in her home; he kept quantities of drugs there, but his dealings were never discussed.

By the time her son had enlisted in the Navy and her daughter had moved to an apartment of her own, Ruth was lonely much of the time. It seemed that John was always gone. She had her job at the employment agency, but after eighteen months even that ended when he insisted she stay at home "where a woman belongs." Arguments became frequent when John *was* there, and one day after a long absence and no word from him, it hit her. What was she doing sitting around stewing in anger when there was a whole drawer full of dope in the house? She could find escape in the euphoria. She opened the drawer and snorted heroin; later she would get her "fix," the needle.

Six months passed before John discovered that Ruth was back on her old habit. He was furious, and the result was an end to their affair.

Then followed Ruth's second arrest. She was on Temple Street once more, looking to score, when she was picked up. She was given two years for parole violation and put back in prison.

When she was released the second time, once more free of her habit, she was hired to work in the narcotics division of the Los Angeles Probation Department. A new program needed former addicts to work as liaisons between the probation officers and drug users. The reasoning was that apprehended addicts always raged at the narcotic officers. Unless they themselves had been hooked, how

216

could cops know what it was like when the biggest, the only, goal in life was the next fix? And so it made sense for the police to hire former addicts who understood, who could reason with those who were hooked.

Ruth was the first woman hired for this program, and she had a hard time landing the job. Living in a halfway house in Hollywood, she applied and was turned down because she did not live in a poverty area.

Her gorge rose. "What do you call living in a halfway house, other than poverty? I don't care if it is at Hollywood and Vine, I haven't any other place to stay."

Years on heroin had taught her how to fight, how to manipulate. The battles were necessary for her very existence. She went to the office of the man who headed the program, and after she had talked to him for ten minutes, he called a subordinate and said, "I want this one. We'll take her."

She tried, she did her level best. But she was once more surrounded in every waking moment by the subject of drugs, unable to divorce herself from the world of the addict. Even after she came home after working on the program, parole officers would phone. "Ruth, have you seen Glenda? We know she's using and want to straighten her out so we don't have to take her back. If you won't tell me where she is, have her call me."

They had used Ruth even when she worked at the employment agency. "Ruth, Alice is out now, and we have no job for her. Will you find a place for her?" And Ruth would get jobs for the addicts until, in their need for a fix, they burglarized a home. Knowing their agony, she went all out in her efforts to help these women. She brought some of them home to her apartment, where they lay on the floor and kicked as their nerves screamed for another fix. She told them, "Look, I've tried. I've done all I can for you. Now it's your turn."

She was attempting to do too much; all her days and

nights were saturated with drugs. So she went back to heroin. The people at the probation department were unaware of it, and for three months Ruth held her job while she was hooked, often sitting in meetings by the hour, hiding the telltale symptoms—and because of her nonconformist nature, experiencing considerable glee in fooling the experts.

At this point in her story, I would guess the reader might lack all sympathy for a woman who repeatedly returned to a dangerous habit, which in its urgency often requires deceit and the committing of crimes in order to support the habit. Without understanding, there is little pity for the sly and furtive addicts who take pleasure in their certainty they are deceiving the world—and who refuse to face the fact they are killing themselves. Perhaps the best way to elicit even a modicum of compassion is to quote Ruth herself:

"I wanted out. Every time I had a fix I wanted to stop. It is fearful to be torn between wanting and not wanting. But I had to have it, had to. Clothes and food meant nothing. If I had a dime as carfare for the three miles to my score, I'd walk out. Because just maybe when I learned the price I'd be a dime short. I lived in terror that the door would be locked, that my supply would be cut off.

"When an addict can't get his fix, his whole body twitches. It's because of the nerves—when the sedative effect of the drug wears off nerves wake and begin screaming for more. I used to lie on the floor with my feet up against a wall so that the blood would run out of my legs and they'd become numb. Anything to stop that jerking, twitching, aching.

"I've been picked up out of the gutters by other addicts. I've lived whole weeks I can't remember.

"There is terror when you're caught. You swallow the stuff, even knowing the balloon might break in your stomach and you will die an agonizing death. But the howling need is always there.

"When you don't get a fix you can't sleep. In jail, without heroin, I went as long as three weeks without closing my eyes. The doctor there said this was impossible, and he put me in the jail hospital to observe my sleeping habits. There weren't any. I stayed awake until he shrugged and said, 'My God, you *can* do it!' I still can't sleep more than three or four hours at a time, and it's been six years since I've had a fix of any kind. I've learned to live without sleep.

"I've hacked it, and I'm one of the few that's left. Nine out of ten people I knew have been found dead, lots of them in alleys."

Back on her habit, she was finally caught by the probation department. Ruth's parole officer came to her room one night at the halfway house and found her "loaded like a dog."

"I'm taking you, Ruth," she said. "Pack your bag. You're going back."

She was in jail again, waiting for the parole board to pronounce sentence once more for violation of parole. It was there she heard that the methadone program begun by the State of California was now accepting women. Methadone is also a drug, but a lighter one, and its beneficial effect is that it kills the desire for heroin. The requirement for acceptance was a felony record, and Ruth had that. From her cell she wrote a letter asking to be put on the program, but she had no response by the time she was released from jail.

This time she was not sent back to the California Institute for Women due to the intervention of the probation department. Because she had done such a good job as a liaison, they wanted her to resume working in that capacity. "Don't send her back. We'll keep her clean. Put her on probation, and we'll take care of her."

They found her an apartment in Burbank, put her back to work, and began such a rigid regimen of checking up that Ruth turned paranoid, certain they'd asked for her services this time only because they wanted to get even with her. She was sure they had no love for her after discovering she had been using heroin under their very noses.

"They had me in their office every single day," she recalls, "And on Saturday and Sunday when the office was closed, they made surprise visits to my apartment. They made damn sure I didn't use anything, because they didn't give me time to get off the bus long enough to go buy it."

They were subsidizing her, but Ruth wanted a real job, a job with a salary of her own, a life of her own. She went to a judge who by then knew her well ("You are a menace," he had once told her) and said she couldn't get or hold a job because the probation department wouldn't free her.

It was settled when, three months after she'd written her letter, she was accepted by the methadone program. Again came a regimented existence. In the state-controlled program it was mandatory that every former heroin addict pick up his or her dose of methadone daily. The "pickup" was in Watts at the southern end of Los Angeles, five buses away from Burbank. The round trip required the better part of every day.

Ruth stuck with it, was a prize pupil, and in less than two years was put on what they called delayed reporting, which required only two trips a week. Each time she was given enough methadone to last until the next trek to Watts. She had no trouble with it, used nothing else, and was perfectly satisfied. Within a period of five years they reduced her dosage from 120 mg. daily to 80 mg.

Ruth herself cut the dosage to 40 mg.—and then blew her top. For a nonconformist, the five years of strict rules had compounded until she could no longer bear the domination. It would be easier, she told herself, to quit altogether. She was tired, drained mentally, physically, and emotionally. At the Watts clinic one day she said, "I won't be back."

They laughed at her, of course. Methadone is addictive, and all addicts come back.

"You want to bet?" she said.

She kept her promise, and it was a giant step, because during the past five years she had complicated her life with a second marriage that had been a disaster. She hadn't loved Steve. She had married him out of the empathy one addict has for another. He wanted to get into the methadone program and could not be accepted unless he was married to a woman already involved in it.

Ruth, by that time in her forties, realized too late it had been a bad bargain. It was a bad marriage, in fact no marriage at all, as he had agreed there would be no consummation. But they lived together, and Steve broke his promise to stay on methadone, taking every kind of drug he could find. At night, after Ruth had retired to her bedroom, Steve entertained his addict friends.

"Stop this," she told him. "I will not have those people in my home."

He turned a deaf ear to her pleas, and one day when she returned from the clinic, she found Steve and a friend arguing violently over a supply of heroin. Disgusted, she went into her bedroom and shut the door and before long heard a resounding thump from the living room. The man had "fallen out" with an overdose, and Steve had grabbed the rest of the heroin and gone into the bathroom to get his fix. He left soon after, paying no attention to the man on the floor. Ruth was scared out of her wits. She dragged the man into the bathroom and propped him up against the tub.

She wanted to call a doctor, but people in the world of drugs do not call doctors, because doctors call the police. Then she remembered a physician at the clinic, a man who just might be lenient. Her hunch was correct; when she phoned him he told her not to worry, that he would not report the incident, but that she should make the man sit up.

"I've already done that," she said. "I propped him against my bathtub."

"Good. If you'd allowed him to lie there his lungs might have filled with fluid." He then told her how to apply ice packs to the man's body—and to pray.

The addict stayed there for three days, out like a light, and Ruth was terrified he might die and she'd be charged with murder.

As soon as the addict regained consciousness, it took Ruth only an hour to pack and leave. She told her husband, "You are not putting me back in the penitentiary. I'm doing well, and if you're not, that's your problem." It *was* his problem; he later died of an overdose.

It was a year after leaving her husband that she told the clinic staff they'd never see her again. But the battle was far from over. To "come down" from methadone, she had gone on codeine, another addictive but still lighter drug in its effect. The years had taken their toll; she was a physical and mental wreck. Doctors hospitalized her several times, and between hospital sieges, she had nothing. There is no way an addict can get and keep a salaried job.

Now hooked on codeine, she went to a psychiatrist at the county mental health department. She wanted out, she wanted off. She was diagnosed as manic depressive, constantly switching between high and low moods. The doctor had her admitted to a mental institution, an incarceration that continued sporadically for many months. There she sat and stared at walls, not eating, not sleeping. Her weight went down to 100 pounds. The doctor decided that shock treatments were the only answer, and needing family permission, sought out Ruth's children. Her daughter came immediately from Denver, where she was living at the time, and when she saw her mother, she was sure Ruth was dying.

"You're coming home with me," she said. She packed Ruth's things and took her back to Denver to live with her.

It was the final stage of kicking the habit. The expression is a literal one; Ruth lay on the couch and kicked.

"Go ahead and kick," her daughter said. "That's all you can do. This is it, mom. Make up your mind to it."

This period of hell was made worse when her daughter's job required her to go on the road. Ruth panicked. She had clung to her daughter, was living for her. If her daughter left her, what would she do?

"You force me to come to Denver, and now you're leaving me," she said. "I'm doing better, sure, but I'm still emotionally unstable. Please don't leave me."

"I have to. Do you want to go back to California?"

"Sure, I want to live in California. I love it, I miss the sea. But I can never live there again. There's too much association, too much temptation. I might go back to using."

In retrospect, Ruth realizes that the separation was the best thing that could have happened. She was again on her way out of addiction, and she summoned the final bit of strength left to her. She would not go back to drugs. Ever. But she had to do something, find a way that would give her back her life. She hadn't had a fix in many months, she felt better, she looked better, she felt a new surge of energy. She joined a group of senior citizens, went to their luncheons, became coordinator for their day trips. But this wasn't enough. She was healthy, she had the will to do something that would fill her days with meaning.

In 1979, having been drug free for three years, she found what she wanted—the Foster Grandparent Program. It has given her the life she needed, wanted.

During the orientation she was taken to visit Ridge, a home for mentally retarded children. Ruth had never seen anything like it, those poor, twisted children with the blank faces, and when a child grabbed her hand so tightly she couldn't free herself, fear surged through her. When they sent her to work at Denver General Hospital, she sighed with relief and sent up a prayer. "Thank you, Jesus."

But at the hospital she met another foster grandparent, eighty-seven-year-old Louise Cowan, who had then worked for the program for thirteen years. Louise talked often of her previous service at Ridge and in particular of a mentally retarded girl of seventeen named Tiffany. Louise Cowan was an inspiration to Ruth, who says, "She's ninety now and still works five days a week—she worked circles around me. She belongs in this book, not me."

Hearing every day about Tiffany, who'd been left on the steps of an orphanage when an infant, Ruth made a decision that has lighted her life.

"I want a transfer," she told the FGP supervisor. "I want to work at Ridge."

"You're sure? We can't get people to work out there. We never have a full quota. Ruth, you're the first person ever to *ask* to work at Ridge."

"I've learned something about myself," Ruth told her. "When I saw Ridge I was frightened, and I thought I was scared of the children. That wasn't it. I was scared of *myself*. I wondered how I could handle it—not how the kids could handle it. I believe I've grown a little bit. I want a permanent child. The kids at the hospital come and go, and I want a permanent child."

At Ridge, they told her she could pick her own child. "I stood against the walls for two weeks," she says, "before I decided maybe I could handle one of those kids, get to know their needs, understand them."

The staff told her, "Choose at your leisure, grandma. Don't rush it."

Louise Cowan's enthusiasm had not gone unheeded, and Ruth observed Tiffany most of the time. Although she had recently turned seventeen, the girl was the size of a ten-year-old. She was confined to a wheelchair, her pale face without expression. If she was in pain tears flowed over her cheeks, but there was no emotion on the face.

Nor was there an expression when she put a foot out

as a staff member came by. Ruth grinned to herself. Now here was a child she could understand, a rebel, an ornery kid right up her alley—it had to take some intelligence to figure out how to trip someone.

Tiffany was a difficult patient, avoided when possible by the staff, because she bit and scratched at anyone who came near her. Tiffany, a victim of the *cri du chat* syndrome, was unable to speak. She had never walked. Her intelligence was rated as that of a three-year-old, and her prognosis was "unteachable." Because of scoliosis, lateral deviation of the spine, she was encased in a heavy brace.

"She had never known love. No one had ever given it to her," says Ruth. "She was a bitter, bitter child, and she was nasty. You can bet your bottom dollar she was nasty. She certainly wasn't the cute little favorite at Ridge."

The staff's most difficult problem with Tiffany was getting fluids into her. Part and parcel of her rebellion was her refusal to drink anything, and the staff had to force liquids into her mouth. Tiffany fought like a tiger, and water would spill over her face, into her eyes and nose.

Ruth decided this was the first obstacle to hurdle. We can go without food for a while, but we must have fluids. She wheeled Tiffany into the dining room after breakfast, when the room was empty and without distraction. She poured a glass of milk for herself and put another in front of the girl.

"We are going to drink," she said.

Each time Tiffany refused, Ruth pulled her from the wheelchair and stood her in a corner, her face to the wall. The girl soon understood this was punishment. After five minutes, Ruth would put her back into the wheelchair and point again to the glass of milk. "Drink it."

The process took months and finally succeeded with the combination of patience and firmness. "I was strict with Tiffy. I believe permissiveness is not caring to a child. Kids believe you don't care if you let them do as they please. A child must have limits. I'm not cruel with her, but I'm consistent. Whenever she disobeyed, I put her in a corner."

The punishment was the same for scratching and hitting. "Pat, like this," said Ruth as she patted Tiffany's arm. "Pat, Don't scratch." Tiffany reached out to scratch once more, and Ruth understood the girl was trying her patience. Up she would go again, propped into the corner, the brace preventing her from falling. By the time Tiffany had ceased attacking people, she was drinking without hesitation. If Ruth drank a Coke, Tiffany drank a Coke; if Ruth drank milk, Tiffany drank milk.

When Ruth arrived one morning, Tiffany looked at her and said something, for the first time in her life. Unable to touch her tongue to the roof of her mouth, she was limited to vowels, and the sound she made sounded like "Oobah."

The fact she'd spoken caused a stir at Ridge. "What's she saying?" wondered Ruth.

"I'll bet it's supposed to be grandma," said a nurse.

It was. Every time Ruth appeared after that, Tiffany said her word—and cried when Ruth left her. Soon another word was added. As a treat when Tiffany had behaved well, Ruth kissed her below the ear.

"That's her joy. When I give her a kiss, she's in hog heaven. Now she smiles and says "ki-ki," which is as close as she can get to the word kiss."

Walking was next. Ruth felt sure that the frequent standing had strengthened Tiffany's legs. She went to the head psychiatrist, told him she thought Tiffany could learn to walk, and asked for suggestions. The doctor brought her a stick, a dowel about two feel long. "Give her one end and hang on to the other. If she falls, don't commiserate, but if she takes a step, hold her in your lap and praise her."

Tiffany took steps, and the staff cheered. She graduated from the dowel to a braided clothesline and took more steps. Then Ruth walked her, holding both her hands, then one hand, finally only a finger. One day Ruth put her in a corner and left to watch from the end of the hall. Tiffany walked along the wall all the way to where she could see Ruth.

"I laughed with joy until I cried," says Ruth. "And I told them that some day she's going to walk out of that corner and come home with me."

It had taken what seemed like eons, but Ruth took Tiffany away from the wall and stood in back of her saying, "Walk, walk. No wall. Keep going."

Early last spring, Tiffany walked, without help from Ruth, across the campus and to the cafeteria with her foster grandmother. On Memorial Day, less than two years after Ruth had begun work with her, Tiffany left the institution for the first time in her life. She went home with Ruth for the weekend. In July, Ruth took her to lunch at a restaurant in Denver.

Tiffany has lost her bitterness and is now a happy child who holds hands with staff members. She laughs as she plays with the balloons Ruth gives her—a spectacular improvement in Ruth's use of balloons.

Currently, Ruth is fighting to get Tiffany admitted to special classes. Soon to turn nineteen, with a deadline of her twenty-first birthday to get an education, the girl has little more than two years left. Ruth insists that Tiffany is now teachable, that she understands everything that's said to her. With typical intensity Ruth says, "I'll get her to those classes if I have to cart her there every day myself. Tiffany has earned the right."

As a ward of the state, Tiffany is eligible to have a citizen advocate, a person to be consulted in decisions such as education and medical care. As you might guess, Ruth has arranged to be the girl's advocate, using every manipulation she learned as a drug addict to fight through bureaucratic red tape and land Tiffany in classes where she can learn everything up to the limit of her potential.

At Ridge they have said, "Ruth, what will you do if they put Tiffany into school eight hours, and you no longer have her as a foster grandchild?"

"Then I'll find a way to get to her on Saturday and Sunday," said Ruth.

Although she does not attend church services, Ruth has never forsaken her early religious training; she says, "Praise the Lord, she's not mine—she was loaned to me. I won't agonize if I lose her. I've grown up enough to know we don't belong to each other, that we both belong to God."

Considering Ruth's remarkable devotion to this child who is not her own, it may well be asked, what of her own children, the son and the daughter whose childhood was filled with sadness, concern, and anger?

Ruth has memories that stab her heart, such as the day she came home with the heroin-filled balloon in her mouth and found not only her son but two policemen waiting for her. She swallowed the stuff surreptitiously, and when the police had left, her son looked at her in disgust and said, "You can spit it out now, mom."

She never lost custody, or track, of her children. She knew always where they were, wrote regularly, visited them on Sundays when they were in a foster home. She made sure they knew where she was at all times, including jail—and "the mental institution with the dazed, crazed souls who had been in Germany's concentration camps and never recovered mentally."

But there is no doubt whatsoever that Ruth's helplessness in addiction was a dark tunnel for her children that left them scarred. It is heartwarming to know that both have always tried to understand and to give what support they could.

Ruth is the first to acknowledge that her persistence with the love of Tiffany, as well as the other children at Ridge, is the result of her guilt about her own children. If she can atone for her past omissions as a mother by making other children happy, perhaps she can erase at least a portion of that guilt.

And yet she considers her work at Ridge a blessing rather than any sort of burden. "Those kids are my life, my sanity, my justification for existence. God took away my dope and knew I had to have something to replace it. He gave me these children." A small, sad smile crosses her face. "When I go to work in the morning and they all yell 'Hi, grandma!'—that is my fix for the day.

"I'm a happy person now. I've never been truly happy in my life until now. I have love now for others and for myself. I can give people dignity; I can smile at people on the street. If a kid gets on a bus and he's going to get kicked off because he doesn't have the fare, I'll put it in for him. During a blizzard I saw a drunk without hat or gloves, and I gave him mine. It was no holy gesture—I could go home that night and look in a mirror and say, Ruth, you're worth something."

She looks down at the half finished afghan in her lap and goes back to plying the crochet needle. As with Tiffany's balloons, this is a much different needle for Ruth, one that allows her to earn income by creating a variety of finely crocheted items.

Now that her friends have learned Ruth's story, I can only hope they will approach her with the same kind of love she is able to give today. For myself, I salute this woman who has come through a long and arduous night of addiction, freed herself from it, and is spending her remaining years in service to others.